Rick Steves®

SNAPSHOT

D0400823

Dublin

CONTENTS

SIGHTS

1. Abbey Theatre
2. Book of Kells & Trinity Old Library
3. Chester Beatty Library
4. Christ Church Cathedral
5. Dublin Castle
6. Dublin City Hall
7. Dublin Writers Museum
8. Dublinia
9. Duke Pub (Literary Pub Crawl)
10. Epic: The Irish Emigration Museum
11. Garden of Remembrance
12. GPO Witness History Exhibit
13. Gogarty's Pub (Musical Pub Crawl)
14. To Guinness Storehouse & Kilmainham Gaol
15. Ha' Penny Bridge
16. Hugh Lane Gallery
17. James Joyce Centre
18. Jeanie Johnston Tall Ship & Famine Museum
19. Little Museum of Dublin
20. Merrion Square
21. National Gallery
22. National Leprechaun Museum
23. National Library
24. National Museum: Archaeology
25. To National Museum: Decorative Arts & History
26. National Museum: Natural History
27. Number 29 Georgian House
28. Old Jameson Distillery & Smithfield Village
29. St. Patrick's Cathedral
30. St. Stephen's Green

Transportation

31. To Airport & M-1 to Belfast
32. Busáras Central Bus Station
33. Connolly Station
34. To Heuston Station

LEGEND

- ▦▦▦ Pedestrian-Friendly Area
- ░░░ Popular Shopping Area
- --- DART Commuter Rail Line
- -T- Red Line LUAS Tram with stops
- -T- Green Line LUAS Tram with stops
- -T- Blue Line LUAS Tram with stops
- ■ Landmark or Point of Interest
- ⊙ Tourist Information

250 Meters

250 Yards

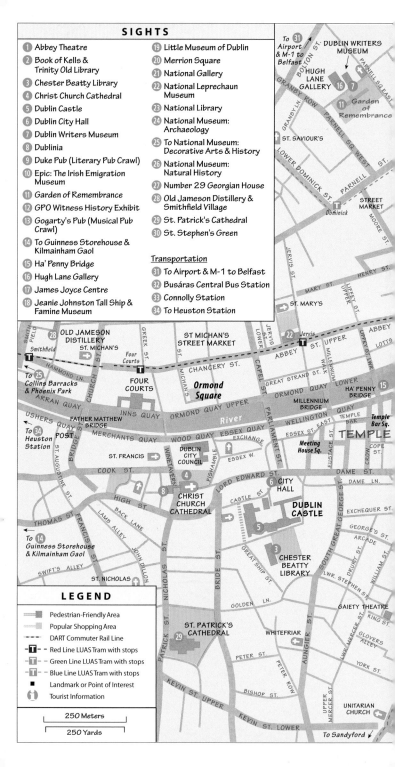

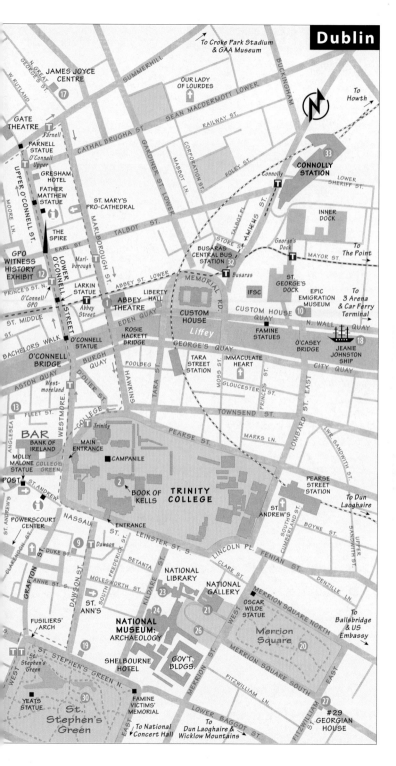

Dublin Restaurants

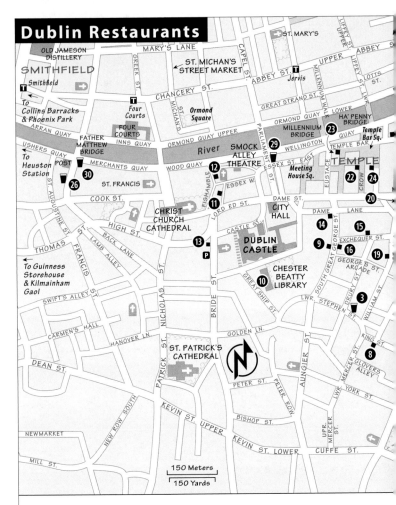

1. Cornucopia
2. The Farm
3. The Hairy Lemon Pub
4. O'Neill's Pub
5. Avoca Café & Sandwich Counter
6. The Duke Pub
7. Davy Byrnes Pub
8. Wagamama & Dunnes Grocery
9. Yamamori
10. Silk Road Café
11. Queen of Tarts
12. Chorus Café
13. Leo Burdock
14. Spar Market
15. Fallon & Byrne Food Hall; Boulevard Café
16. Dunnes Grocery
17. Marks & Spencer

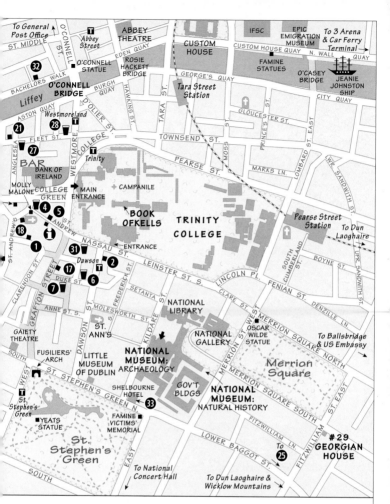

18 Trocadero

19 Eden Bar & Grill

20 The Bank

21 Gallagher's Boxty House

22 Luigi Malone's

23 The Shack

24 Bad Ass Café

25 To Grand Canal Eateries

26 The Brazen Head Pub

27 Gogarty's Pub

28 Palace Bar

29 Porterhouse

30 O'Shea's Merchant Pub

31 Dingle Whiskey Bar

32 Arlington Hotel (Celtic Show)

33 The Shelbourne Hotel
(Afternoon Tea)

INTRODUCTION

This Snapshot guide, excerpted from my guidebook *Rick Steves Ireland*, introduces you to the city of Dublin. From its lively pubs filled with Guinness-fueled *craic* (conversation) and traditional music, to its stately Georgian sights, to its powerful rebel history, the Irish capital delights its visitors. Stroll vibrant O'Connell Street for a lesson in Ireland's long struggle for independence, cheer on the local hurling team at Croke Park, and pore over the intricately decorated ninth-century Book of Kells. Pious, earthy, witty, brooding, feisty, and unpretentious, Dublin is an intoxicating potion to sip or slurp—as the mood strikes you.

For a break from the big city, venture to sights near Dublin: the prehistoric tombs at Brú na Bóinne, the site of the pivotal Battle of the Boyne, the stout ruins of Trim Castle, the impressive Gardens of Powerscourt, the monastic settlement at Glendalough, and the proud Irish equestrian tradition at the National Stud.

To help you have the best trip possible, I've included the following topics in this book:

- **Planning Your Time,** with advice on how to make the most of your limited time

- **Orientation,** including tourist information (abbreviated as TI), tips on public transportation, local tour options, and helpful hints

- **Sights** with ratings:

  ▲▲▲—Don't miss

  ▲▲—Try hard to see

  ▲—Worthwhile if you can make it

  No rating—Worth knowing about

- **Sleeping** and **Eating,** with good-value recommendations in every price range

• **Connections,** with tips on trains, buses, and driving

Practicalities, near the end of this book, has information on money, staying connected, hotel reservations, transportation, and more.

To travel smartly, read this little book in its entirety before you go. It's my hope that this guide will make your trip more meaningful and rewarding. Traveling like a temporary local, you'll get the absolute most out of every mile, minute, and dollar.

Happy travels!

DUBLIN

With reminders of its stirring history and rich culture on every corner, Ireland's capital and largest city is a sightseer's delight. Dublin punches above its weight class in arts, entertainment, food, and fun. The vibe is infectious and by the time you depart, Dublin's fair city will have you humming, "Cockles and mussels, alive, alive-O."

Founded as a Viking trading settlement in the ninth century, Dublin grew to be a center of wealth and commerce, second only to London in the British Empire. As the seat of English rule in Ireland for 750 years, Dublin was the heart of a "civilized" Anglo-Irish area (eastern Ireland) known as "the Pale." Anything "beyond the Pale" was considered uncultured and almost barbaric...purely Irish.

The Golden Age of English Dublin was the 18th century. The British Empire was on a roll, and the city was right there with it. Largely rebuilt during this Georgian era, Dublin became an elegant and cultured capital.

Those glory days left a lasting imprint on the city. Squares and boulevards built in the Georgian style, such as Merrion Square, give the city an air of grandeur ("Georgian" is British for Neoclassical...named for the period when four consecutive King Georges occupied the British throne from 1714 to 1830). The National Museum, the National Gallery, and many government buildings are in the Georgian section of town.

Throughout the 19th century, as Ireland endured the Great Potato Famine and saw the beginnings of the modern struggle for independence, Dublin was treated—and felt—more like a British colony than a partner. The tension culminated in the Easter Rising of 1916, followed by a successful guerilla war of independence against Britain and Ireland's tragic civil war. With many of its grand streets in ruins, war-torn Dublin emerged as the capital of the British Empire's only former colony in Europe.

While bullet-pocked buildings and dramatic statues keep memories of Ireland's struggle for independence alive, the city is looking ahead to a brighter future. In the last decade, the tentative "green shoots" of a hoped-for financial recovery from the devastating 2008 crash have sprouted into a forest of cranes sweeping over booming construction blocks and expanding light rail infrastructure. Dubliners are energetic and helpful, and visitors enjoy a big-town cultural scene wrapped in a small-town smile.

PLANNING YOUR TIME

This bustling city is a must for travelers interested in Celtic/Viking artifacts, Irish literature, or rebel history. For most people, Dublin deserves three nights and two days.

Be aware that some important sights close on Mondays. Reserve Kilmainham Gaol in advance or risk it being sold out. Consider this ambitious sightseeing plan:

Day 1

9:00   Visit the Book of Kells and Old Trinity Library ahead of mid-morning crowds.

11:00   Take the guided Historical Walking Tour.

12:30   Browse Grafton Street, have lunch there, or picnic on St. Stephen's Green.

14:00   Head to the National Museum: Archaeology branch (closed Mon).

16:00   Visit Epic: The Irish Emigration Museum.

17:30   Return to hotel, rest, have dinner.

19:30   Go for an evening guided pub tour (musical or literary).

22:00   If you still have the energy, find a pub with live Irish music.

Day 2

9:00   Tour Kilmainham Gaol (reserve ahead; opens at 9:30 Sept-May).

11:00   Take the Dublin Castle tour.

13:00   Grab lunch.

14:30   Follow the self-guided "O'Connell Street Stroll" in this chapter, taking in the GPO Witness History exhibit en route (in the General Post Office).

Evening Options: Catch a concert, a play, the storytelling dinner at The Brazen Head (or one of the other recommended dinner shows), another guided pub tour (musical or literary), or more live folk music in a pub.

Orientation to Dublin

Greater Dublin sprawls with well over a million people—more than a quarter of the country's population. But the center of tourist interest is a tight triangle between O'Connell Bridge, St. Stephen's Green, and Christ Church Cathedral. Within or near this triangle, you'll find Trinity College (Book of Kells), a cluster of major museums (including the National Museum: Archaeology), touristy and pedestrianized Grafton Street, Temple Bar (touristy nightlife center), Dublin Castle, and the hub of most city tours and buses. The major sights outside this easy-to-walk triangle are the General Post Office ("GPO" to locals; north of the center), and Kilmainham Gaol and the Guinness Storehouse (west of the center).

The River Liffey cuts the town in two, and most of your sightseeing will take place on its south bank. Many long Dublin streets change names every few blocks, including the wide main axis that cuts north/south through the tourist center. North from the O'Connell Bridge, it's called O'Connell Street; south of the bridge, it becomes Westmoreland, passes Trinity College, and becomes the pedestrian-only Grafton Street to St. Stephen's Green.

Two suburbs, Dun Laoghaire to the south and Howth to the north, offer quiet home-base alternatives to Dublin (with easy 25-minute transit connections into town). By staying outside the city, you'll save about 25 percent on your hotel costs.

TOURIST INFORMATION

Dublin's busy main TI has lots of info and brochures on Dublin and all of Ireland (Mon-Sat 9:00-17:30, Sun 10:30-15:00, a block off Grafton Street at 25 Suffolk Street, tel. 01/884-7700, www. visitdublin.com). A smaller but equally helpful TI is just past the Spire, on the east side of O'Connell Street (Mon-Sat 9:00-17:00, closed Sun). Watch out for other shops that claim to be TIs, especially on O'Connell Street. They're aiming to sell you tours and collect commissions.

Dublin Pass: This sightseeing pass covers 25 sights and landmarks (but not the Book of Kells), hop-on, hop-off buses, and the Aircoach airport bus—one-way from the airport to the city only (pass—€52/1 day, multiday options available, purchase online and collect at TIs, www.dublinpass.ie). If you already have the Heritage Card, skip this one, as the card already covers two big Dublin sights (Kilmainham Gaol and Dublin Castle).

DUBLIN

Maps: At any TI, you can pick up the free *Dublin Pocket Guide*, but the best free city map is the one created by the Kilkenny Shop (6 Nassau Street, bordering the south side of the Trinity College campus)—available at tourist outlets throughout the city.

ARRIVAL IN DUBLIN

For details on Dublin's airport, as well as ferry connections between the UK and Dublin, see "Dublin Connections," at the end of this chapter.

By Train: Dublin has two train stations. Heuston Station, on the west end of town, serves west and southwest Ireland (45-minute walk from O'Connell Bridge; take the LUAS light rail or bus #90—see below). Connolly Station, which serves the north, northwest, and Rosslare, is closer to the center (15-minute walk from O'Connell Bridge). Each station has ATMs but no lockers.

The train stations are connected by the red line of the LUAS light-rail system and by bus #90, which runs along the river (€2, 4/hour). From the city center, to reach Heuston Station, catch bus #90 on the south side of the river; to get to Connolly Station and Busáras Central Bus Station, catch #90 on the north side of the river.

By Bus: Bus Éireann, Ireland's national bus company, uses the Busáras Central Bus Station (pronounced bu-SAUR-us). Located next to Connolly Station, it's a 10-minute walk or a short ride on bus #90 to the city center.

By Car: Don't drive in downtown Dublin—traffic's terrible, parking is expensive, and there are plenty of smarter options. If you have to park in central Dublin, a good option is Q-Park Christ Church, on Werburgh Street behind Jurys Inn Christ Church (€3.50/hour, €16/day, tel. 01/454-9001).

HELPFUL HINTS

Pickpockets: Irish destinations, especially Dublin, are not immune to this scourge. Be on guard—use a money belt or carefully zip things up.

Festivals: Book ahead during festivals and for any weekend. **St. Patrick's Day** is a four-day March extravaganza in Dublin (www.stpatricksday.ie). June 16 is **Bloomsday,** dedicated to the Irish author James Joyce and featuring the Messenger Bike Rally (www.jamesjoyce.ie). Hotels raise their prices and are packed on rugby weekends (about four per year), during

DUBLIN

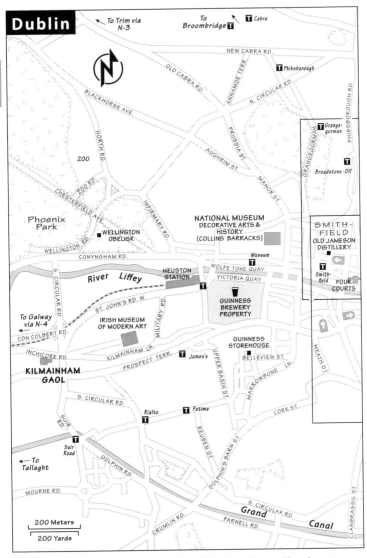

the all-Ireland Gaelic football and hurling finals (Sundays in
September), and during summer rock concerts.

Meet a Dubliner: The **City of a Thousand Welcomes** offers a free
service that brings together volunteers and first-time visitors.
Sign up online in advance and pick an available time slot.
In Dublin you'll meet your "ambassador," head for a nearby
tearoom or pub, and enjoy a drink (paid for by the city) and
a friendly, informal conversation (of up to an hour). It's a
great way to get oriented to the city (meet at Little Museum

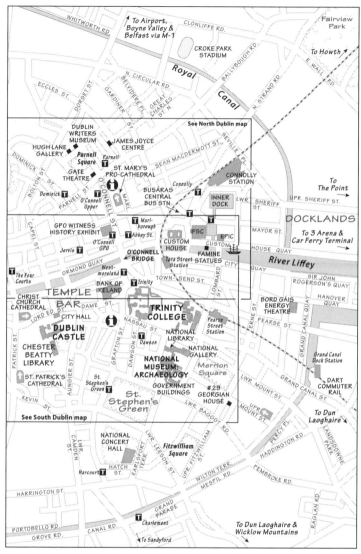

of Dublin, 15 St. Stephens Green, tel. 01/661-1000, www. cityofathousandwelcomes.com).

Mass in Latin: The Roman Catholic Mass is said in Latin daily at St. Kevin's Church (Mon-Fri at 8:00, Sat at 9:00, Sun at 10:30, corner of Harrington and Synge, about six blocks south of St. Patrick's Cathedral, www.latinmassdublin.ie).

Bookstores: The giant granddaddy of them all is **Eason's,** five minutes north of the O'Connell Bridge (Mon-Sat 8:00-19:00,

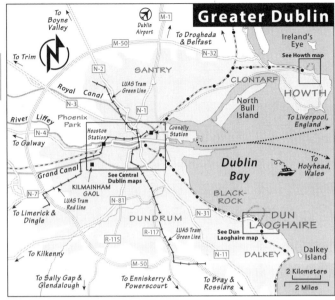

Sun 12:00-18:00, 40 O'Connell Street Lower, tel. 01/858-3800, www.easons.com).

Laundry: Krystal Launderette, a block southwest of Jurys Inn Christ Church on Patrick Street, offers same-day full service (Mon-Sat 8:00-20:00, Sun 12:00-17:00, tel. 01/454-6864). The **All-American Launderette** offers self- and full-service options (Mon-Sat 8:30-19:00, Sun 10:00-18:00, 40 South Great George's Street, tel. 01/677-2779).

Bike Rental: River Cycles is right along the south side of the River Liffey on Usher's Island quay, about four blocks west of The Brazen Head pub. From here, consider a low-stress ride into the huge, bike-friendly Phoenix Park (€4/2 hours, €5/4 hours, €10/day, daily 10:00-19:00 "weather depending," 10 Usher's Island, mobile 086-265-6258, www.rivercyclesphoenixparkbikehire.com).

GETTING AROUND DUBLIN

You'll do most of Dublin on foot, though when you need public transportation, you'll find it readily available and easy to use. With a little planning, sightseers can make excellent use of a two-day hop-on, hop-off bus ticket to link the best sights. Also, keep in mind that (for cross-city travel) the expanding LUAS light-rail system does not get bogged down in traffic like buses and taxis do.

By Public Transportation

You can buy individual tickets for the bus, DART, and LUAS, or get a transit card that can be used on all three (described below).

Bus: Public buses are cheap and cover the city thoroughly. Most lines start at the four quays (riverfront streets) that are nearest O'Connell Bridge. If you're away from the center, nearly any bus takes you back downtown. Some bus stops are "request only" stops: Be alert to the bus numbers (above the windshield) of approaching buses, and when you see your bus coming, flag it down. Tell the driver where you're going, and he'll ask for €2-3.30 depending on the number of stops. Bring coins, as drivers don't make change.

The Dublin Bus office has free route maps and sells the transit cards described below (Mon-Fri 9:00-17:30, Sat-Sun 9:30-14:00, 59 Upper O'Connell Street, tel. 01/873-4222, www.dublinbus.ie).

DART Train: Speedy commuter trains run along the coast, connecting Dublin with suburban Dun Laoghaire (south) and Howth (north). Think of the DART line as a giant "C" that serves coastal suburbs from Bray in the south up to Howth (€3.25, €6.15 round-trips valid same day only, buy at machine, 4/hour, tel. 01/703-3504, www.irishrail.ie/home).

LUAS Light Rail: The city's light-rail system has two main lines, red and green. The most useful for tourists is the red line, with an east-west section connecting the Heuston and Connolly train stations (15-minute ride apart) at opposite edges of the Central 1 Zone; in between, the Busáras, Smithfield, and Museum stops can be handy. Useful north-south green line stops are at St. Stephen's Green, Trinity College, and both ends of O'Connell Street (€2, buy at machine, 6/hour, runs until 24:45, tel. 1-800-300-604, www.luas.ie). Monitors at each boarding platform display the time and end destination of the next LUAS train; check to make sure you're on the right platform for the direction you want to go.

Transit Cards: The **Leap Card** is good for travel on Dublin's bus, DART, and LUAS routes, and fares are lower than buying individual tickets. Leap Cards are sold at TIs, newsstands, and markets citywide—look for the leaping-frog logo—and can be topped up (€5 refundable deposit, www.leapcard.ie).

For those staying in Dun Laoghaire or Howth—or on a long-term stay in Dublin—the **Leap Visitor Card** may be a better option. It enables unlimited travel on Dublin's buses (including Airlink Express to and from the airport), DART, and LUAS trams (€10/1 day, €19.50/3 days, €40/7 days, each "day" equals 24 hours from first use, http://about.leapcard.ie/leap-visitor-card). It's possible to buy the card online in advance, but it's just as easy to pick one up at the airport (transportation desk in Terminal 1 or at the Spar in Terminal 2) or from several Dublin city center locations (main TI, Dublin Bus office, or Discover Ireland Centre at 14 Upper O'Connell Street).

The **Do Dublin** transit and discount card covers the Airlink Express, public buses in Dublin, and the Do Dublin hop-on, hop-off bus, while offering some sight discounts. Purchase in advance online, at the Do Dublin airport desk (Terminal 1), or the Dublin Bus office (€33/72 hours, tel. 01/844-4265, www.dodublin.ie).

By Taxi or Uber

Taxis are everywhere and easy to hail. Cabbies are generally honest, friendly, and good sources of information (drop charge—€3.60 daytime, €4 nighttime, €1/each additional adult, figure about €12-15 for most crosstown rides, €40/hour for guided joyride).

Your Uber app will get you two choices in Dublin: "Uber" is actually a taxi (with the standard metered rate, but no tipping and billed to your account); "Uber Black" is an expensive chauffeur-driven car.

Tours in Dublin

While Dublin's physical treasures are lackluster by European standards, the gritty city has a fine story to tell and people with a natural knack for telling it. It's a good town for walking tours, and competition is fierce. Pamphlets touting creative walks are posted all over town. Choices include medieval walks, literary walks, Georgian Dublin walks, and traditional music or literary pub crawls. Taking an evening walk is a great way to meet other travelers. The Dublin TI also offers a variety of free, good-quality, downloadable "Dublin Discovery Trails" audio tours.

ON FOOT
▲▲Historical Walking Tour

This is your best introductory walk. A group of hardworking history graduates enliven Dublin's basic historic strip (Trinity College, Old Parliament House, Dublin Castle, and Christ Church Cathedral). You'll get the story of their city, from its Viking origins to the present. Guides speak at length about the roots of Ireland's struggle with Britain. As you listen to your guide, you'll stand in front of buildings that aren't much to look at, but are lots to talk about (April-Oct daily at 11:00, May-Sept also at 15:00; Nov-March Fri-Sun at 11:00). All walks last 90 minutes and cost €12 (ask for discount with this book, free for kids under 14, departs from front gate of Trinity College, private tours available, mobile 087-688-9412 or 087-830-3523, www.historicalinsights.ie).

▲▲Traditional Irish Musical Pub Crawl

This entertaining tour visits the upstairs rooms of three pubs; there, you'll listen to two musicians talk about, play, and sing traditional

Irish music. While having only two musicians makes the music a bit thin (Irish music aficionados will say you're better off just finding a good session), the evening—though touristy—provides a real education in traditional Irish music. The musicians clearly enjoy introducing rookies to their art and are very good at it. And they are really funny. In the summer, this popular 2.5-hour tour frequently sells out, but it's easy to reserve ahead online (€14, ask for discount with this book—use code RSIRISH online, beer extra, at 19:30 April-Oct daily, Jan-March Thu-Sat only, no shows Dec, maximum 65 people, meet upstairs at Gogarty's Pub at the corner of Fleet and Anglesea in the Temple Bar area, tel. 01/475-3313, www.musicalpubcrawl.com). They also offer a dinner-show version.

Dublin Literary Pub Crawl

Two actors take 40 or so tourists on a walk, stopping at four pubs, and with clever banter introduce the high *craic* of James Joyce, Seán O'Casey, and W. B. Yeats. The two-hour tour is punctuated with 20-minute pub breaks (free time). This is an easygoing excuse to drink beer in busy pubs, meet other travelers, and get a dose of Irish witty lit (€13, at 19:30 April-Oct daily, Nov-March Thu-Sun only; just show up, but reserve ahead in July-Aug when it can fill up; meet upstairs in the Duke Pub—off Grafton on Duke Street, tel. 01/670-5602, mobile 087-263-0270, www.dublinpubcrawl.com). Connoisseurs of Irish pubs enjoy the excellent *Dublin Literary Pub Crawl* guidebook by pub-crawl founder Colm Quilligan.

1916 Rebellion Walking Tour

This two-hour walk breathes gritty life into the most turbulent year in modern Irish history, when idealistic Irish rebels launched the Easter Rising—eventually leading to independence from Britain. Guide Lorcan Collins has written a guidebook called *The Easter Rising*—worth seeking out—and is passionate about his walks (€13, ask for discount with this book; March-Oct Mon-Sat at 11:30, Sun at 13:00; Nov-Feb Fri-Sun at 11:30; departs from International Bar at 23 Wicklow Street, mobile 086-858-3847, www.1916rising.com).

Pat Liddy's Walking Tours

Pat Liddy, one of Dublin's top historians, and his guides take groups on enthusiastic and informal two-hour walks of hidden Dublin districts. Unlike most Dublin walks, this one does a good job of covering the often overlooked but historic north side of town. His "Highlights and Hidden Corners" tour starts near the General Post Office building, winds down across the river to City Hall, through Temple Bar, and ends at Trinity College (€12, April-Oct daily at 11:00, no tours Sun, Tue, or Thu in off-season, meet in front of Dublin Bus office at 59 Upper O'Connell Street, tel. 01/832-9406, mobile 087-905-2480, www.walkingtours.ie).

Local Guides

Two proud Dubliners will show you around town when they're not on the road leading Rick Steves tours: **Joe Darcy** is a friendly guy with a passion for Irish literature, who enjoys unpeeling the urban layers of his hometown for visitors (€120 for up to 4 people for 2.5-hour walking tour, mobile 086-218-0357, josdarcy@gmail.com). Witty **Dara McCarthy** offers similar services for the same rates (mobile 087-291-6798, dara@daramccarthy.com).

BY BIKE

Dublin City Bike Tours

You'll "get your *craic* on a saddle" with Dublin City Bike Tours as you pedal across this flat city on a fun, innovative tour that covers five miles and visits 20 points of interest north and south of the River Liffey. Designed for riders of average fitness, they set a casual pace, and rarely let a little rain stop them (€27 includes bike, helmet, snack, and water; ask for discount with this book; cash only, reserve in advance, 2.5 hours; March-Nov daily at 10:00, additional tours Fri and Sat at 14:00; departs Isaac's Hostel a half-block west of Busáras bus station at 2 Frenchman's Lane, mobile 087-134-1866, www.dublincitybiketours.com).

Lazy Bike Tour Company

For a less strenuous option, you can grab a bright orange electric bike and matching vest, and buzz along on a guided tour that covers sights from Dublin Castle to Kilmainham Gaol. Tours start in Temple Bar and last two hours (€30, daily at 10:00, 12:30, and 15:00; book in advance in summer; meet at 4 Scarlet Row on Essex Street West in Temple Bar near Christ Church Cathedral, 01/443-3671, www.lazybiketours.com).

BY BUS (ON LAND AND WATER)

▲Hop-on, Hop-off Bus Tours

Taking a hop-on, hop-off bus tour is an excellent way to orient yourself on arrival in Dublin. Several companies running roofless double-deckers do similar 1.5-hour circuits of the city (up to 30 stops, buses circle every 10-15 minutes daily 9:00-17:00, usually until 19:00 in summer). This type of tour, with running commen-

taries (either live or recorded), is made-to-order
for Dublin, and buses run
so frequently that they
make your sightseeing su-
per-efficient. Stops include
the far-flung Guinness
Storehouse and Kilmain-
ham Gaol. Each company

offers various discounts to museums and sights in town, and two
kids ride free with each adult.

Do Dublin (green buses) has drivers who provide fun and
quirky narration, and your ticket includes free entry into the Little
Museum of Dublin and a free walking tour from Pat Liddy's Walking Tours (€19/24 hours, €23/48 hours, tel. 01/703-3028, www.
dublinsightseeing.ie).

Dublin CityScape (yellow buses) offers three routes (€15/24
hours, €18/72 hours, tel. 01/465-9972, http://cityscapetours.ie).

City Sightseeing Dublin (red buses) has a handy "blue
route" that takes you as far as Glasnevin Cemetery and Croke
Park (€19/24 hours, €25/48 hours, tel. 01/898-0700, https://
citysightseeingdublin.ie). They also offer a 90-minute musical **evening tour** (without stops) with a live guide who narrates but also
sings and plays guitar (€10, June-Sept nightly at 20:00 and 21:30,
buy ticket from driver, leaves from the Gresham Hotel at 14 Upper
O'Connell Street).

▲Viking Splash Tours

If you'd like to ride in a WWII-amphibious vehicle—driven by a
Viking-costumed guide who spouts jokes and historic factoids as
you ramble through town—this is it. The tour starts with a group
roar from the Viking within us all. At first, the guide talks as if he
were a Viking ("When we came here in 841..."), but soon the patriot emerges as he tags Irish history onto the sights you pass. Near
the end of the 75-minute tour (punctuated by occasional group
roars at passersby), you take a slow spin up and down a boring canal
(€22, Feb-Nov daily 10:00-17:00, no tours Dec-Jan, departs about
hourly from the north side of St. Stephen's Green opposite Dawson Street, buy ticket from driver, dress warmly, tel. 01/707-6000,
www.vikingsplash.com).

TOUR PACKAGES FOR STUDENTS

Andy Steves (Rick's son) runs Weekend Student Adventures
(WSA Europe), offering 3-day and 10-day budget travel packages
across Europe including accommodations, skip-the-line sightseeing, and unique local experiences. Locally guided and DIY options

Dublin at a Glance

▲▲▲National Museum: Archaeology Interesting collection of Irish treasures from the Stone Age to today. **Hours:** Tue-Sat 10:00-17:00, Sun from 14:00, closed Mon. See page 28.

▲▲▲Kilmainham Gaol Historic jail used by the British as a political prison—today a museum that tells a moving story of the suffering of the Irish people. **Hours:** Guided tours daily June-Aug 9:00-18:45, Sept-May 9:30-17:30. See page 54.

▲▲▲Book of Kells in the Trinity Old Library An exquisite illuminated manuscript, Ireland's most important piece of art from the Dark Ages. **Hours:** May-Sept Mon-Sat 8:30-17:00, Sun from 9:30; Oct-April Mon-Sat 9:30-17:00, Sun 12:00-16:30. See page 24.

▲▲Historical Walking Tour Your best introduction to Dublin. **Hours:** April-Oct daily at 11:00, May-Sept also at 15:00; Nov-March Fri-Sun at 11:00. See page 12.

▲▲Traditional Irish Musical Pub Crawl A fascinating, practical, and enjoyable primer on traditional Irish music. **Hours:** April-Oct daily at 19:30, Nov and Jan-March Thu-Sat only. See page 13.

▲▲Chester Beatty Library American expatriate's sumptuous collection of literary and religious treasures from Islam, Asia, and medieval Europe. **Hours:** Mon-Fri 10:00-17:00, Sat from 11:00, Sun from 13:00; closed Mon Nov-Feb. See page 39.

▲▲GPO Witness History Exhibit Immersive presentation on the 1916 Easter Rising and its impact on Irish history, situated in the building that served as the rebel headquarters. **Hours:** Mon-Fri 9:00-17:30, Thu until 19:00 in July-Aug, Sat-Sun 10:00-17:30. See page 51.

▲▲Temple Bar Dublin's rowdiest neighborhood, with shops, cafés, theaters, galleries, pubs, and restaurants—a great spot for live (but touristy) traditional music. See page 44.

▲▲Trinity College Tour Ireland's most famous school, best visited with a 30-minute tour led by one of its students. **Hours:** Departs every 30 minutes daily 9:15-16:00, Feb-April and Oct-Nov Sat-Sun only. See page 24.

▲▲O'Connell Street Dublin's grandest promenade and main drag, packed with history and ideal for a stroll. See page 18.

▲▲Epic: The Irish Emigration Museum Creative displays about the Irish diaspora that highlight the emigrants' influences on their new homelands. **Hours:** Daily 10:00-18:45. See page 45.

▲**Dublin Castle** The city's historic 700-year-old castle, featuring ornate English state apartments (interior tourable only with a guide). **Hours:** Mon-Sat 10:00-16:45, Sun from 12:00. See page 38.

▲**Guinness Storehouse** The home of Ireland's national beer, with a museum of beer-making, a gallery of clever ads, and Gravity Bar with panoramic city views. **Hours:** Daily 9:30-19:00, July-Aug until 20:00. See page 55.

▲**National Gallery of Ireland** Fine collection of top Irish painters and European masters. **Hours:** Mon-Sat 9:30-17:30, Thu until 20:30, Sun 11:00-17:30. See page 33.

▲**Jeanie Johnston Tall Ship and Famine Museum** Floating exhibit on the River Liffey explaining the Famine period that prompted desperate transatlantic crossings (by tour only). **Hours:** Daily April-Sept 10:00-16:00, Oct-March 11:00-15:00. See page 46.

▲**Grafton Street** The city's liveliest pedestrian shopping street. See page 37.

▲**St. Stephen's Green** Relaxing park surrounded by fine Georgian buildings. See page 37.

▲**Dublinia** A fun, kid-friendly look at Dublin's Viking and medieval past with a side order of archaeology and a cool town model. **Hours:** Daily 10:00-18:30, Oct-Feb until 17:30. See page 42.

▲**Merrion Square** Enjoyable and inviting park with a fun statue of Oscar Wilde. See page 36.

▲**Hugh Lane Gallery** Modern and contemporary art, starring Monet, Bacon, and Irish artists. **Hours:** Tue-Thu 10:00-18:00, Fri-Sat until 17:00, Sun 11:00-17:00, closed Mon. See page 49.

▲**Dublin Writers Museum** Connoisseur's collection of authorial bric-a-brac. **Hours:** Mon-Sat 9:45-17:00, Sun from 11:00. See page 46.

▲**National Museum: Decorative Arts and History** Shows off Irish dress, furniture, silver, and weaponry with a special focus on the 1916 rebellion, fight for independence, and civil war. **Hours:** Tue-Sat 10:00-17:00, Sun from 14:00, closed Mon. See page 57.

▲**Gaelic Athletic Association Museum** High-tech museum of traditional Gaelic sports (hurling and Irish football). **Hours:** Mon-Sat 9:30-17:00, June-Aug until 18:00, Sun 10:30-17:00 year-round. On game Sundays, it's open to ticket holders only. See page 57.

are available for student and budget travelers in 13 of Europe's most popular cities, including Dublin (guided trips from €199, see www.wsaeurope.com for details). Check out Andy's tips, resources, and podcast at www.andysteves.com.

O'Connell Street Stroll

This self-guided walk, worth ▲▲, follows Dublin's grandest street from the O'Connell Bridge through the heart of north Dublin. Since the 1740s, the street has been a 45-yard-wide promenade, and ever since the first O'Connell Bridge connected it to the Trinity side of town in 1794, it's been Dublin's main drag. (It was named O'Connell only after independence in 1922.) These days, the city has made the street more pedestrian-friendly, and a LUAS line runs along the median. Though lined with touristy fast-food joints and souvenir shops, O'Connell Street echoes with history.

• *Start your walk on the...*

❶ **O'Connell Bridge:** This bridge—actually wider than it is long—spans the River Liffey, which historically has divided the wealthy, cultivated south side of town from the working-class north side. While there's plenty of culture on the north bank, even today the suburbs (a couple of miles north of the Liffey) are considered rougher and less safe. Dubliners joke that "north-siders" are known as "the accused," while "south siders" are addressed as "your honor."

From the bridge, look as far upstream (west) as you can. On the left in the distance, the concrete building before the green dome marks the birthplace of the city. It squats on the still-buried site of the first Viking settlement, established in Dublin in the ninth century. On the right side of the river, a pleasant boardwalk leads upriver to the elegant iron Ha' Penny Bridge. That bridge leads into the Temple Bar nightlife district (on the left).

Turn 180 degrees and look downstream (east) to see the tall Liberty Hall union headquarters (16 stories tall, some say in honor of the 1916 Easter Rising). Modern Dublin is developing downstream. During the Celtic Tiger boom in the mid-1990s, the Irish subsidized and revitalized this formerly dreary quarter. While "the Tiger" died with the great recession of 2008-2009, Dublin's economy is booming again—as illustrated by the forest of cranes marking building sites in the east end of town.

A short walk downstream along the north bank leads to a powerful series of gaunt statues memorializing the Great Potato Famine of 1845-1849. Beyond, you'll see the masts of the *Jeanie Johnston*, a replica transport ship.

• *Now start north up O'Connell Street, walking on the wide, tree-lined median strip toward the spike in the sky.*

Statues and Monuments: Ireland's history is celebrated all

DUBLIN

O'Connell Street Stroll

To Airport & M-1 to Belfast

DUBLIN WRITERS MUSEUM

HUGH LANE GALLERY

WALK ENDS

Pool

Garden of Remembrance

JAMES JOYCE CENTRE

To Croke Park Stadium & GAA Museum

GATE THEATRE

Parnell

SUMMERHILL

CATHAL BRUGHA ST.

O'Connell Upper

ST. MARY'S PRO-CATHEDRAL

STREET MARKET

150 Meters
150 Yards

TALBOT ST.

Marlborough

EARL ST.

SACKVILLE PLACE

GPO WITNESS HISTORY EXHIBIT

O'Connell GPO

ABBEY ST. LOWER

ABBEY THEATRE

PRINCE'S ST. NORTH

Abbey Street

LUAS Tram Red Line

ABBEY ST. MIDDLE

Jervis

ABBEY ST. UPPER

NORTH LOTTS ST.

EDEN QUAY

ROSIE HACKETT BRIDGE

Liffey

BURGH QUAY

GREAT STRAND ST.

BACHELORS WALK

O'CONNELL BRIDGE

WALK BEGINS

River

To Temple Bar

HA' PENNY BRIDGE

ASTON QUAY

Westmoreland

To Trinity College

HAWKINS ST.

- ❶ O'Connell Bridge
- ❷ Daniel O'Connell Statue
- ❸ William Smith O'Brien Statue
- ❹ Abbey Theatre
- ❺ Sir John Gray Statue
- ❻ James Larkin Statue
- ❼ General Post Office & Witness History Exhibit
- ❽ The Spire
- ❾ Moore Street Market
- ❿ St. Mary's Pro-Cathedral
- ⓫ Father Matthew Statue
- ⓬ Gresham Hotel
- ⓭ Charles Stewart Parnell Monument
- ⓮ Gate Theatre
- ⓯ Garden of Remembrance
- ⓰ Dublin Writers Museum
- ⓱ Hugh Lane Gallery
- ⓲ James Joyce Centre

along O'Connell Street. The median is dotted with statues remembering great figures from Ireland's past—particularly the century (c.1830-1930) when Ireland rediscovered its roots and won its independence. At the base of the street stands the man for whom Dublin's main street is named—❷ **Daniel O'Connell** (1775-1847). He was known as the "Liberator" for founding the Catholic Association and demanding Irish Catholic rights in the British Parliament. He organized thousands of nonviolent protestors into "monster meetings," whose sheer size intimidated the British authorities.

Farther along is ❸ **William Smith O'Brien**, O'Connell's contemporary and leader of the Young Ireland Movement, who was more willing to use force to reach his goals. After a failed uprising in Tipperary, he was imprisoned, sentenced to death in 1848, but then exiled to Australia.

At Abbey Street, a one-block detour to the east (right) leads to the famous ❹ **Abbey Theatre,** where turn-of-the-century nationalists (including the poet-playwright W. B. Yeats) staged Irish-themed plays. The original building suffered a fire and was rebuilt into a nondescript, modern building, but it's still the much-loved home of the Irish National Theatre.

• *Continue up O'Connell Street.*

Look for the statue of ❺ **Sir John Gray,** who, as a newspaperman and politician, was able to help O'Connell's cause. The statue of ❻ **James Larkin,** arms outstretched, honors the founder of the Irish Transport Workers Union.

• *On your left is the...*

❼ **General Post Office (GPO):** This is not just any P.O. It was from here that Patrick Pearse read the Proclamation of Irish Independence in 1916, kicking off the Easter Rising. The building itself—a kind of Irish Alamo—was the rebel headquarters and scene of a bloody five-day siege that followed the proclamation. The post office was particularly strategic because it housed the telegraph nerve center for the entire country. Its pillars are still pockmarked with bullet holes. The engaging GPO Witness History exhibit, on your right as you go inside, brings the dramatic history of this important building to life.

• *Arch way back (at the intersection of O'Connell and Henry streets) and marvel up at...*

❽ **The Spire:** There used to be a monument here that didn't wave an Irish flag—a tall column crowned by a statue of the Brit-

DUBLIN

ish hero of Trafalgar, Admiral Horatio Nelson. It was blown up in 1966—the IRA's contribution to the local celebration of the Easter Rising's 50th anniversary. The spot is now occupied by the Spire: 398 feet of stainless steel. While it trumpets rejuvenation on its side of the river, it's a memorial to nothing and has no real meaning. Dubliners call it the tallest waste of €5 million in all of Europe. Its nickname? Take your pick: the Stiletto in the Ghetto, the Stiffy on the Liffey, the Pole in the Hole, or the Poker near the Croker (after nearby Croke Park). The "erection at the intersection" was built for the millennium, but Dublin was only able to get it up by 2004. Before leaving, have fun standing close and looking way up.

• *Detour a block west (left) down people-filled Henry Street (Dubliners' favorite shopping lane), then wander to the right into the nearby...*

❾ **Moore Street Market:** Many merchants here have staffed the same stalls for decades (Mon-Sat 8:00-18:00, closed Sun). Start a conversation. It's a great workaday scene. You'll see lots of mums with strollers—a reminder that Ireland is one of Europe's youngest countries, with about 35 percent of the population under the age of 25. At the end of the 1916 Easter Rising, the rebel leaders retreated from the burning post office to #16 on this street, where they finally surrendered to British troops (see plaque high up).

• *Return to O'Connell Street. A block east (right) of O'Connell, down Cathedral Street, detour to...*

❿ **St. Mary's Pro-Cathedral:** Although this is Dublin's leading Catholic church, it isn't a cathedral but a "pro-cathedral" (as in "provisional")—essentially a parish church serving temporarily as a cathedral. The pope declared Christ Church to be a cathedral in the 12th century—and later, gave St. Patrick's the same designation (and they remain "cathedrals" even though they haven't been Catholic for centuries).

St. Mary's sits on the site of the 12th-century Abbey of St. Mary. With the Reformation leading to Henry VIII's dissolution of the monasteries in 1539, the abbey's "popish trappings" were tossed out and the land confiscated.

In the 18th century, with Catholic worship legal but better done with a low profile, a modest Catholic "Mass house" opened on Liffey Street. Church fathers, however, envisioned a bold new St. Mary's on the main street (where the GPO is today), but they eventually backed away from that high-profile location, and instead built this Neoclassical church here (completed 1825). It's set back from the action, with no big steeple or fancy facade—looking more like a bomb shelter than a dignified church. An unhappy alteration to increase the church's capacity caused it to grow with an odd floor plan. Don't miss the fine Victorian windows (behind the altar) dating from the 1880s. For two centuries, St. Mary's has been part of the stage upon which Irish history has played out:

Daniel O'Connell gave a rousing speech here in 1825 at its dedication, and later lay in state here in 1847. It hosted the funeral Mass of Michael Collins in 1922, and Éamon de Valera (a leader of the Easter Rising) also lay in state here in 1975.

• *Back on O'Connell Street, head up the street (north) until you find the statue of...*

❶ **Father Matthew:** A leader of the temperance movement of the 1830s, Father Matthew was responsible, some historians claim, for enough Irish peasants staying sober to enable Daniel O'Connell to organize them into a political force.

Nearby, the fancy ❷ **Gresham Hotel** is a good place for an elegant tea or beer. In an earlier era, the beautiful people alighted here during visits to Dublin.

• *Standing boldly at the top of O'Connell Street is a monument to...*

❸ **Charles Stewart Parnell:** Ringing the monument are the names of the four ancient provinces of Ireland and all 32 Irish counties (north and south, since this was erect-

ed before Irish partition). It's meant to honor Charles Stewart Parnell (1846-1891), the member of Parliament who nearly won Home Rule for Ireland in the late 1800s (and who served time at Kilmainham Gaol). A Cambridge-educated Protestant of landed-gentry stock, Parnell envisioned a modern, free Irish nation of Catholics—but not as a religious state. The Irish people, who remembered their grandparents' harsh evictions during the Fam-ine, came to love Parnell (despite his privileged birth) for his tireless work to secure fair rents and land tenure. Momentum seemed to be on his side. With the British prime minister of the time, William Gladstone, favoring a similar form of Home Rule, it looked as if Ireland was on its way toward independence as a Commonwealth nation, similar to Canada or Australia.

Then a sex scandal broke around Parnell and his mistress, the wife of another Parliament member. The press, egged on by the powerful Catholic bishops (who didn't want a secular, free Irish state), battered away at the scandal until finally Parnell was driven from office. Wracked with exhaustion and only in his mid-40s, Parnell died brokenhearted.

After that, Ireland became mired in the conflicts of the 20th century: an awkward independence (1921) featuring a divided is-land, a bloody civil war, and sectarian violence for decades after-ward.

• *Continue uphill, straight up Parnell Square East. At the* ❹ *Gate The-atre (on the left), actors Orson Welles, Geraldine Fitzgerald, and James*

Mason had their professional stage debuts. One block up, on the left, is the...

⓯ **Garden of Remembrance:** Honoring the victims of the 1916 Rising, this spot was where the rebel leaders were held before being transferred to Kilmainham Gaol. The park was dedicated in 1966 on the 50th anniversary of the revolt that ultimately led to Irish independence. The bottom of the cross-shaped pool is a mosaic of Celtic weapons, symbolic of how the early Irish proclaimed peace by breaking their weapons and throwing them into a lake or river. The Irish flag flies above the park: green for Catholics, orange for Protestants, and white for the hope that they can live together in peace (park open daily 8:30-18:00).

One of modern Ireland's most stirring moments occurred here in May 2011, when Queen Elizabeth II made this the first stop on her historic visit to Ireland. She laid a wreath at the *Children of Lir* sculpture under this flag and bowed her head in silence out of respect for the Irish rebels who had fought and died trying to gain freedom from her United Kingdom. This was a hugely cathartic moment for both nations. Until this visit, no British monarch had set foot in the Irish state since its founding 90 years earlier.

• *Your walk is over. Two excellent museums are nearby, standing side-by-side: the ⓰ Dublin Writers Museum (in a splendidly restored Georgian mansion) and the art-filled ⓱ Hugh Lane Gallery. Here at the north end of town, it's also convenient to visit the ⓲ James Joyce Centre (a short walk away), or the Gaelic Athletic Association Museum at Croke Park Stadium (a 20-minute walk or short taxi ride away). Otherwise, hop on your skateboard and zip back to the river.*

Sights in Dublin

SOUTH OF THE RIVER LIFFEY
Trinity College

Founded in 1592 by Queen Elizabeth I to establish a Protestant way of thinking about God, Trinity has long been Ireland's most prestigious college. Originally, the student body was limited to rich Protestant men. Women were admitted in 1903, and Catholics—though allowed entrance by the school much earlier—were given formal permission by the Catholic Church to study at Trinity in the 1970s (before that they risked excommunication). Today, half of Trinity's 12,500 students are women, and 70 percent are culturally Catholic (although only about 20 percent of Irish youth are church-going).

Combo-Ticket: There are two worthwhile sights here—a half-hour tour of the grounds led by students and the Book of Kells in the library. If you are considering both, the €14 combo-ticket is a screaming deal considering the Book of Kells admission alone is €13. Buy the ticket at the college gate (see details below).

▲▲Trinity College Tour

Trinity students lead 30-minute tours of their campus (look just inside the gate for posted departure times and a ticket seller on a stool). You'll get a rundown of the mostly Georgian architecture;

a peek at student life past and present; and the enjoyable company of your guide, a witty Irish college kid.

Cost and Hours: €6, €14 combo-ticket also covers Book of Kells (where the tour leaves you), cash preferred; tours run daily 9:15-16:00, Sat-Sun only in Feb-April and Oct-Nov, no tours Dec-Jan; tours depart roughly every 30 minutes, weather permitting, https://www.tcd.ie/visitors/tours/.

▲▲▲Book of Kells in the Trinity Old Library

The Book of Kells—a 1,200-year-old version of the four gospels—was elaborately inked and meticulously illustrated by faithful monks. Combining Christian symbols and pagan styles, it's a snapshot of medieval Ireland in transition. Arguably the finest piece of art from what is generally called the Dark Ages, the Book of Kells shows that monastic life in this far fringe of Europe was far from dark.

Cost and Hours: €13, €10 off-peak ticket is good before 10:00 and after 15:00, €14 combo-ticket also covers tour—see details above; May-Sept Mon-Sat 8:30-17:00, Sun from 9:30; Oct-April Mon-Sat 9:30-17:00, Sun 12:00-16:30; audioguide-€5, tel. 01/896-2320, www.tcd.ie/visitors/book-of-kells.

Crowd-Beating Tips: Lines are longest at midday (roughly 10:00-15:00). Those with online tickets skip the queue. To have the Book of Kells all to yourself, be there at opening.

Background: The Book of Kells was a labor of love created by dedicated Irish monks cloistered on the remote Scottish island of Iona. They slaughtered 185 calves, soaked the skins in lime, scraped off the hair, and dried the skins into a cream-colored writing surface called vellum. Only then could the tonsured monks pick up their swan-quill pens and get to work.

The project may have been underway in 806 when Vikings savagely pillaged and burned Iona, killing 68 monks. The survivors fled to the Abbey of Kells (near Dublin). Scholars debate exactly where the book was produced: It could have been made entirely at Iona or at Kells, or started in Iona and finished at Kells.

For eight centuries, the glorious gospel sat regally atop the high altar of the monastery church at Kells, where the priest would read from it during special Masses. In 1654, as Cromwell's puritanical rule settled in, the book was smuggled to Dublin for safety. Here at Trinity College, it was first displayed to the public in the mid-1800s. In 1953, the book got its current covers and was bound into four separate volumes.

Visiting the Book of Kells: Your visit has three stages: 1) an exhibit on the making of the Book of Kells, including poster-sized reproductions of its pages (your best look at the book's detail); 2) the Treasury, the darkened room containing the Book of Kells itself and other, less ornate contemporaneous volumes; and, upstairs, 3) the Old Library (called the Long Room), containing historical objects.

The Exhibit: The first-class "Turning Darkness into Light" exhibit, with a one-way route, puts the illuminated manuscript in its historical and cultural context, preparing you to see the original book and other precious manuscripts in the treasury. Make a point to spend time in the exhibit (before reaching the actual Book of Kells). Especially interesting are the short, continuously running video clips that show the ancient art of bookbinding and the exacting care that went into transcribing the monk-uscripts. Don't miss these as they vividly show the skill and patience needed for the monks' work.

The Book: The Book of Kells contains the four gospels of the Bible (typically only two of the gospels are on display at any given time). Altogether, it's 680 pages long (or 340 "folios," the equivalent of one sheet, front and back). The Latin calligraphy—all in capital letters—follows ruled lines, forming neat horizontal bars across the page. Sentences end with a "period" of three dots. The black-brown ink was made from the galls of oak trees.

The text is elaborately decorated—of the hundreds of pages, only two are without illustration. Each gospel begins with a full-page depiction of the Evangelists and their symbols: Matthew (angel), Mark (lion), Luke (ox), and John (eagle). The apostles pose stiffly, like Byzantine-style icons, with almond-shaped eyes and

DUBLIN

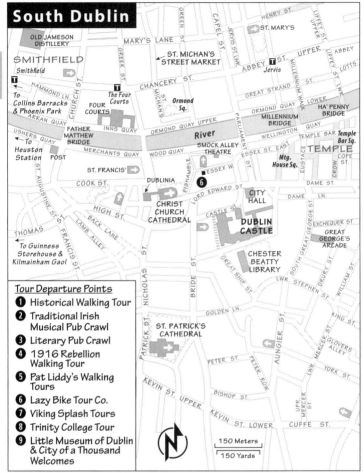

South Dublin

Tour Departure Points
1 Historical Walking Tour
2 Traditional Irish Musical Pub Crawl
3 Literary Pub Crawl
4 1916 Rebellion Walking Tour
5 Pat Liddy's Walking Tours
6 Lazy Bike Tour Co.
7 Viking Splash Tours
8 Trinity College Tour
9 Little Museum of Dublin & City of a Thousand Welcomes

150 Meters
150 Yards

symmetrically creased robes. The true beauty lies in the intricate designs that surround the figures.

The colorful book employs blue, purple, red, pink, green, and yellow pigments (all imported)—but no gold leaf. Letters and borders are braided together. On most pages, the initial letters are big and flowery, like in a children's fairytale book.

Notice how the playful monks might cross a "t" with a fish, form an "h" from a spindly-legged man, or make an "e" out of a coiled snake. Animals crouch between sentences. It's a jungle of intricate designs, inhabited by tiny creatures both real and fanciful.

Scholars think three main artists created the book: the "goldsmith" (who did the filigree-style designs), the "illustrator" (who specialized in animals and grotesques), and the "portrait painter"

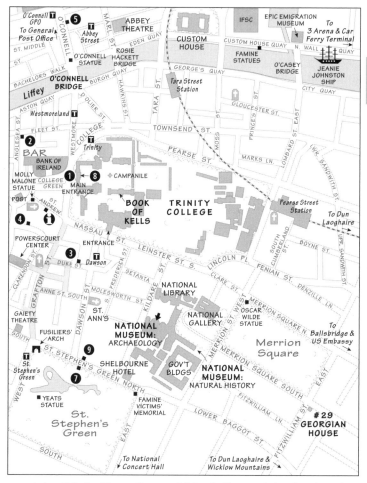

(who did the Evangelists and Mary). Some of the detail work is unbelievably minute.

The Old Library: The Long Room, the 200-foot-long main chamber of the Old Library (from 1732), is stacked to its towering ceiling with 200,000 books. Among the displays here, you'll find one of a dozen surviving original copies of the Proclamation of the Irish Republic. Patrick Pearse read out its words at Dublin's General Post Office on April 24, 1916, starting the Easter Rising that led to Irish independence. Notice the inclusive opening phrase ("Irishmen and Irishwomen") and the seven signatories (each of whom was later executed).

Another national icon is nearby: the oldest surviving Irish harp, from the 15th century (sometimes called the Brian Boru harp, although it was crafted 400 years after the death of this Irish king). The brass pins on its oak and willow frame once held 29 strings. In Celtic days, poets—highly influential with kings and druid priests—wandered the land, uniting the people with songs and stories. The harp's inspirational effect on Gaelic culture was so strong that Queen Elizabeth I (1558-1603) ordered Irish harpists to be hung and their instruments smashed. Even today, the love of music is so intense that Ireland is the only country with a musical instrument as its national symbol. You'll see this harp's likeness on the back of Irish euro coins, on government documents, and (respectfully reversed) on every pint of Guinness.

▲▲▲National Museum: Archaeology

Showing off the treasures of Ireland from the Stone Age to modern times, this branch of the National Museum is itself a national treasure. The soggy marshes and peat bogs of Ireland have proven perfect for preserving old objects. You'll see 4,000-year-old gold jewelry, 2,000-year-old bog mummies, 1,000-year-old Viking swords, and the collection's superstar—the exquisitely wrought Tara Brooch. Visit here to get an introduction to the rest of Ireland's historic attractions: You'll find a reconstructed passage tomb like Newgrange, Celtic art like the

Book of Kells, Viking objects from Dublin, a model of the Hill of Tara, and a sacred cross from the Cong Abbey. Hit the highlights of my tour, then browse the exhibits at will, all well-described throughout.

Cost and Hours: Free, Tue-Sat 10:00-17:00, Sun from 14:00, closed Mon, €3 audioguide covers only Treasury room, good café, between Trinity College and St. Stephen's Green on Kildare Street, tel. 01/677-7444, www.museum.ie.

➲ Self-Guided Tour

• *On the ground floor, enter the main hall and get oriented (with the help of this book's map): In the center (down four steps) are displays of prehistoric gold jewelry. To the left are the bog bodies, to the right is the Treasury, and upstairs is the Viking world. We'll start at Ireland's beginning.*

❶ **Stone Age Tools:** Glass cases hold flint and stone ax-heads and arrowheads (7,000 B.C.). Ireland's first inhabitants—hunters and fishers who came from Scotland—used these tools. These early people also left behind standing stones (dolmens) and passage tombs.

❷ **Reconstructed Passage Tomb:** At the corner of the room,

DUBLIN

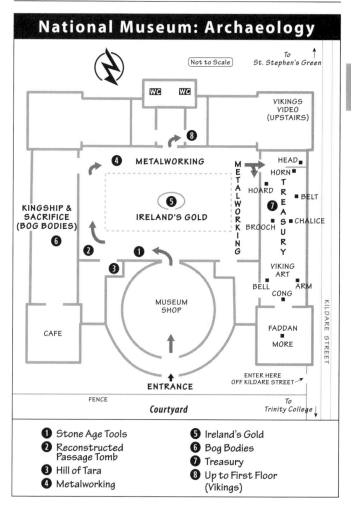

National Museum: Archaeology

Not to Scale

To
St. Stephen's Green

WC   WC

VIKINGS
VIDEO
(UPSTAIRS)

4 METALWORKING

HEAD ■
HORN ■

M
E
T
A
L
W
O
R
K
I
N
G

HOARD ■

T
R
E
A
S
U
R
Y

■ BELT

7

5
IRELAND'S GOLD

BROOCH ■

■ CHALICE

KINGSHIP &
SACRIFICE
(BOG BODIES)

6

2

1

VIKING
ART

3

BELL ■   ■ ARM
CONG ■

KILDARE STREET

MUSEUM
SHOP

CAFE

FADDAN
■
MORE

ENTER HERE
OFF KILDARE STREET ↗

ENTRANCE

FENCE

Courtyard

To
Trinity College ↓

1 Stone Age Tools
2 Reconstructed
   Passage Tomb
3 Hill of Tara
4 Metalworking

5 Ireland's Gold
6 Bog Bodies
7 Treasury
8 Up to First Floor
   (Vikings)

you'll see a typical tomb circa 3,000 B.C.—a mound-shaped, heavy stone structure, covered with smaller rocks, with a passage leading into a central burial chamber where the deceased's ashes were interred. This is a modest tomb; the vast passage tombs at Newgrange and Knowth are similar but many times bigger.

❸ The Hill of Tara: The famous passage-tomb burial site at Tara, known as the Mound of the Hostages, was used for more than 1,500 years as a place to inter human remains. The cases in this side gallery display some of the many exceptional Neolithic and Bronze Age finds uncovered at the site.

Over the millennia, the Mound became the very symbol of Irish heritage. This is where Ireland's kings claimed their power, where St. Patrick preached his deal-clinching sermon, and where, in 1843, Daniel O'Connell rallied Irish patriots to demand their independence from Britain (see illustration in poster on the left wall).

❹ **The Evolution of Metalworking:** Around 2500 B.C., Ireland discovered how to make metal—mining ore, smelting it in furnaces, and casting or hammering it into shapes. The rest is prehistory. You'll travel through the Bronze Age (ax-heads from 2000 B.C.) and Iron Age (500 B.C.) as you examine assorted spears, shields, swords, and war horns. The cauldrons made for everyday cooking were also used ceremonially to prepare elaborate ritual feasts for friends and symbolic offerings for the gods. The most impressive metal objects are four steps down in the center of the hall.

❺ **Ireland's Gold:** Ireland had only modest gold deposits, mainly gathered by prehistoric people panning for small nuggets and dust in the rivers. But the jewelry they left, some of it more than 4,000 years old, is exquisite. The earliest fashion choice was a broad necklace hammered flat (a *lunula,* so called for its crescent-moon shape). This might be worn with accompanying earrings and sun-disc brooches. The Gleninsheen Collar (c. 700 B.C.) was found by a farmer in a crevice of the exposed bedrock of the Burren. It's thought that this valuable status symbol was hidden there during a time of conflict, then forgotten (or its owner killed)—if it had been meant as an offer-

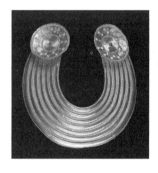

ing to a pagan god it more likely would have been left in a body of water (the portal to the underworld). Later Bronze Age jewelry was cast from clay molds into bracelets and unique "dress fasteners" that you'd slip into buttonholes to secure a cloak. Some of these gold objects may have been gifts to fertility gods, offered by burying them in marshy bogs.

❻ **Bog Bodies:** When the Celts arrived in Ireland (c. 500 B.C.-A.D. 500), they brought with them a mysterious practice: They brutally murdered sacrificial slaves or prisoners and buried them in bogs. Four bodies (each in its own tiny theater with a description outside)—shriveled and leathery, but remarkably preserved—have been dug up from around the Celtic world.

Clonycavan Man is from Ireland. One summer day around 200 B.C., this twenty-something man was hacked to death with an ax and disemboweled. In his time, he stood 5'9" tall and had a Mohawk-style haircut, poofed up with pine-resin hair product imported from France. Today you can still see traces of his hair. Only his upper body survived; the lower part may have been lost in the threshing machine that unearthed him in 2003.

Why were these people killed? It appears to have been a form of ritual human sacrifice of high-status people. Some may have been enemy chiefs or political rivals. The sacrifices could have been offerings to the gods to ensure rich harvests and good luck. Other items (now on display) were buried along with them—gold bracelets, royal cloaks, and finely wrought cauldrons.

❼ **Treasury:** Irish metalworking is legendary, and this room holds 1,500 years of exquisite objects. Working from one end of the long room to the other, you'll journey from the world of the pagan Celts to the coming of Christianity, explore the stylistic impact of the Viking invasions (9th-12th century), and consider the resurgence of ecclesiastical metalworking (11th-12th century).

Pagan Era Art: The carved stone head of a mysterious pagan god greets you (#19, circa A.D. 100). The god's three faces express the different aspects of his stony personality. This abstract style—typical of Celtic art—would be at home in a modern art museum. A bronze horn (#17, first century B.C.) is the kind of curved war trumpet that Celts blasted to freak out the Roman legions on the Continent (the Romans never invaded Ireland). The fine objects of the Broighter Hoard (#15, first century B.C.) include a king's golden collar decorated in textbook Celtic style, with interlaced vines inhabited by stylized faces. The tiny boat was an offering to the sea god. The coconut-shell-shaped bowl symbolized a cauldron. By custom, the cauldron held food as a constant offering to Danu, the Celtic mother goddess, whose mythical palace was at Brú na Bóinne.

Early Christian Objects: Christianity officially entered Ireland in the fifth century (when St. Patrick converted the pagan king), but Celtic legends and art continued well into the Christian era. You'll see various crosses, shrines (portable reliquaries containing holy relics), and chalices decorated with Celtic motifs. The Belt Shrine (#32)—a circular metal casing that held a saint's leather belt—was thought to have magical properties. When placed around someone's waist, it could heal the wearer or force him or her to tell the truth.

The Ardagh Chalice (#30) and the nearby Silver Paten (#31) were used during Communion to hold blessed wine and bread. Get close to admire the elaborate workmanship. The main bowl of the chalice is gilded bronze, with a contrasting band of intricately patterned gold filigree. It's studded with colorful glass, amber, and enamels. Mirrors below the display case show that even the underside of the chalice was decorated. When the priest grabbed the chalice by its two handles and tipped it to his lips, the base could be admired by God.

DUBLIN

Tara Brooch: A rich eighth-century Celtic man fastened his cloak at the shoulder with this elaborate ring-shaped brooch (#29), its seven-inch stickpin tilted rakishly upward. Made of cast and gilded silver, it's ornamented with fine, exquisitely filigreed gold panels and studded with amber, enamel, and colored glass. The motifs include Celtic spirals, snakes, and stylized faces, but the symbolism is neither overtly pagan nor Christian—it's art for art's sake. Despite its name, the brooch probably has no connection to the Hill of Tara. In display cases nearby, you'll see other similar (but less impressive) brooches from the same period—some iron, some bronze, and one in pure gold.

Viking Art Styles: When Vikings invaded Dublin around A.D. 800, they raped and pillaged. But they also opened Ireland to a vast and cosmopolitan trading empire, from which they imported hoards of silver (see the display case of ingots). Viking influence shows up in the decorative style of reliquaries like the Lismore Crozier (#43, in the shape of a bishop's ceremonial shepherd's crook) and the Shrine of St. Lochter's Arm (raised in an Irish-power salute). The impressive Bell of St. Patrick (#24) was supposedly owned by Ireland's patron saint. After his death, it was encased within a beautifully worked shrine (displayed above) and kept safe by a single family, who passed it down from generation to generation for 800 years.

Cross of Cong: "By this cross is covered the cross on which the Creator of the world suffered." Running along the sides of the cross (#44), this Latin inscription tells us that it once held a sacred relic, a tiny splinter of the True Cross on which Jesus was crucified. That piece of wood (now lost) had been given in 1123 to the Irish high king, who commissioned this reliquary to preserve the splinter (it would have been placed right in the center, visible through the large piece of rock crystal). Every Christmas and Easter, the cross was fitted onto a staff and paraded through the abbey at Cong, then placed on the altar for High Mass. The extraordinarily detailed decoration features gold filigree interspersed with colored glass, enamel, and (now missing) precious stones. Though

fully Christian, the cross has Celtic-style filigree patterning and Viking-style animal heads (notice how they grip the cross in their jaws).

Before leaving the Treasury, enter the room behind the Cross of Cong and check out the Faddan More Psalter—a (pretty beat-up) manuscript of the Book of Psalms from the same era as the Book of Kells.

• *Now head up to the first floor to the Viking world. Start in the long hall directly above the Treasury, with the informative 25-minute video on the Viking influence on Irish culture.*

❽ **Viking Ireland** (c. 800-1150): Dublin was born as a Viking town. Sometime after 795, Scandinavian warriors rowed their long ships up the River Liffey and made camp on the south bank, around the location of today's Dublin Castle and Christ Church. Over the next two centuries, they built "Dubh linn" ("black pool" in Irish) into an important trading post, slave market, metalworking center, and the first true city in Ireland. (See a model of Dublin showing a recently excavated area near Kilmainham Gaol.)

The state-of-the-art Viking boats worked equally well in the open ocean and shallow rivers, and were perfect for stealth invasions and far-ranging trading. Soon, provincial Dublin was connected with the wider world—Scotland, England, northern Europe, even Asia. The museum's displays of swords and spears make it clear that, yes, the Vikings were fierce warriors. But you'll also see that they were respected merchants (standardized weights and coins), herders and craftsmen (leather shoes and bags), fashion-conscious (bone combs and jewelry), fun-loving (board games), and literate (runic alphabet). What you won't see are horned helmets, which, despite the stereotype, were not Viking. By 1050, the pagan Vikings had intermarried with the locals, become Christian, and were melting into Irish society.

• *With time and interest, you could explore the...*

Rest of the Museum: Part of the ground floor is dedicated to medieval Ireland—daily life (ploughs, cauldrons), trade (coins, pottery), and religion (crucifixes and saints). Up one more flight, the Egyptian room has coffins, *shabtis,* and canopic jars—but no mummies.

Other National Museums South of Trinity College

Adjacent to the archaeology branch are these other major museums. Also nearby is Leinster House. Once the Duke of Leinster's home, it now hosts the Irish Dáil (parliament) and Seanad (senate), which meet here 90 days each year.

▲National Gallery of Ireland

While not as extensive as national galleries in London or Paris, the collections here are well worth your time. The beautifully renovated museum boasts an impressive range of works by European masters and displays the works of top Irish painters, including Jack B. Yeats (brother of the famous poet).

Cost and Hours: Free, Mon-Sat 9:30-17:30, Thu until 20:30,

DUBLIN

Modern Ireland's Turbulent Birth:
A Timeline

Imagine if our American patriot ancestors had fought both our Revolutionary War and our Civil War over a span of seven chaotic years...and then appreciate the remarkable resilience of the Irish people. Here's a summary of what happened when.

Easter Rising, 1916: A nationalist militia called the Volunteers (led by **Patrick Pearse**) and the socialist Irish Citizen Army (led by **James Connolly**) join forces in the Easter Rising, but they fail to end 750 years of British rule. The uprising is unpopular with most Irish, who are unhappy with the destruction in Dublin and preoccupied with the "Great War" on the Continent. But when 16 rebel leaders (including Pearse and Connolly) are executed, Irish public opinion reverses as sympathy grows for the martyrs and the cause of Irish Independence.

Two important rebel leaders escape execution. Brooklyn-born **Éamon de Valera** is spared because of his American passport (the British don't want to anger their potential ally in World War I). **Michael Collins,** a low-ranking rebel officer who fought in the Rising at the General Post Office, refines urban guerrilla-warfare strategies in prison, and then blossoms after his release as the rebels' military and intelligence leader in the power vacuum that followed the executions.

General Election, 1918: World War I ends and a general election is held in Ireland (the first in which women can vote). Outside of Ulster, the nationalist **Sinn Fein** party wins 73 out of 79 seats in Parliament. Only four out of 32 counties vote to maintain the Union with Britain (all four lie in today's Northern Ireland). Rather than take their seats in London, Sinn Fein representatives abstain from participating in a government they see as foreign occupiers.

War of Independence, 1919: On January 19, the abstaining Sinn Fein members set up a rebel government in Dublin called Dáil

Sun 11:00-17:30, Merrion Square West, tel. 01/661-5133, www.nationalgallery.ie.

Tours: Take advantage of the free audioguide (donations accepted) as well as free 45-minute guided tours (Sat at 12:30; Sun at 12:30 and 13:30).

Visiting the Museum: Be sure to walk through the series of rooms on the ground floor devoted to Irish painting and get to know artists you may not have heard of before. Visit the National

Éireann. On the same day, the first shots of the Irish War of Independence are fired as rebels begin ambushing police barracks, which are seen as an extension of British rule. De Valera is elected by the Dáil to lead the rebels, with Collins as his deputy. Collins' web of spies infiltrates British intelligence at Dublin Castle. The Volunteers rename themselves the **Irish Republican Army;** meanwhile the British beef up their military presence in Ireland by sending in tough WWI vets, the Black and Tans. A bloody and very personal war ensues.

Anglo-Irish Treaty, 1921: Having lived through the slaughter of World War I, the British tire of the extended bloodshed in Ireland and begin negotiations with the rebels. De Valera leads rebel negotiations, but then entrusts them to Collins (a clever politician, De Valera sees that whoever signs a treaty will be blamed for its compromises). Understanding the tricky position he's been placed in, Collins signs the Anglo-Irish Treaty in December, lamenting that in doing so he has signed his "own death warrant."

The Dáil narrowly ratifies the treaty (64 to 57), but Collins' followers are unable to convince De Valera's supporters that the compromises are a stepping-stone to later full independence. De Valera and his antitreaty disciples resign in protest. **Arthur Griffith,** founder of Sinn Fein, assumes the presidential post.

Irish Civil War, 1921: In June, the antitreaty forces, holed up in the Four Courts building in Dublin, are fired upon by Collins and his protreaty forces—thus igniting the Irish Civil War. The British want the treaty to stand and even supply Collins with cannons, meanwhile threatening to reenter Ireland if the antitreaty forces aren't put down.

Aftermath, 1922/23: In August 1922, Griffith dies of stress-induced illness, and Collins is assassinated 10 days later. Nevertheless, the protreaty forces prevail, as they are backed by popular opinion and better (British-supplied) military equipment.

By April 1923, the remaining IRA forces dump (or stash) their arms, ending the civil war...but many bitter IRA vets vow to carry on the fight. De Valera distances himself from the IRA and becomes the dominant Irish political leader for the next 40 years.

Portrait Gallery on the mezzanine level for an insight into the great personalities of Ireland. You'll find European masterworks on the top floor, including a rare Vermeer (one of only 30-some known works by the Dutch artist), a classic Caravaggio (master of chiaroscuro and dramatic lighting), a Monet riverscape, and an early Cubist Picasso still life.

Perhaps the most iconic of all the Irish art in this museum is the melodramatic (and huge) c. 1854 depiction of the *Marriage of Strongbow and Aiofe* by Daniel Maclise. It captures the chaotic union of Norman and Irish interests that signaled the start of English domination of Ireland 850 years ago. Notice how the defeated Irish writhe and lament in the bright light of the foreground, while the scheming Norman warlords skulk in the dimly lit middle ground. The ruins of conquered Waterford smolder at the back.

National Museum: Natural History

Called "the dead zoo" by Dubliners, this cramped collection of stuffed exotic animals comes across like the locker room on Noah's Ark. But if you're into beaks, bones, bugs, and boars, this Victorian relic is for you. Standing tall above a sea of taxidermy is the regal skeleton of a giant Irish elk from the last Ice Age; it dwarfs a modern moose.

Cost and Hours: Free, Tue-Sat 10:00-17:00, Sun from 14:00, closed Mon, Merrion Square West, tel. 01/677-7444, www.museum.ie.

National Library of Ireland

Literature holds a lofty place in the Irish psyche. To feel the fire-and-ice pulse of Ireland's most influential poet, visit the W. B. Yeats exhibit in the library basement. The artifacts flesh out the very human passions of this poet and playwright, with samples of his handwritten manuscripts and surprisingly interesting mini documentaries of the times he lived in. Upstairs, you can get help making use of library records to trace your genealogy. Take a moment to view the gorgeous baby-blue upstairs reading room under the expansive dome.

Cost and Hours: Free, Mon-Wed 9:30-19:30, Thu-Fri until 16:30, Sat until 12:30, Sun 13:00-16:30, café, tel. 01/603-0200, 2 Kildare Street, www.nli.ie.

Merrion Square and Nearby
▲Merrion Square

Laid out in 1762, this square is ringed by elegant Georgian houses decorated with fine doors—a Dublin trademark. (If you're inspired by the ornate knobs and knockers, there's a shop by that name on nearby Nassau Street.) The park, once the exclusive domain of the residents (among them, Daniel O'Connell at #58 and W. B. Yeats at #82), is now a delightful public escape and ideal for a picnic. To learn what "snogging" is, walk through the park on a sunny day, when it's full of smooching lovers. Oscar Wilde, lounging wittily on a boulder on the corner nearest the

town center and surrounded by his clever quotes, provides a fun photo op.

▲Number Twenty-Nine Georgian House

The carefully restored house at Number 29 Lower Fitzwilliam Street gives an intimate glimpse of middle-class Georgian life—but is closed for renovation until 2020 (tel. 01/702-6163, www.esb.ie/no29).

Grafton Street and St. Stephen's Green Area

▲Grafton Street

Once filled with noisy traffic, today's Grafton Street is Dublin's liveliest pedestrian shopping drag and people-watching paradise. A 10-minute stroll past street musicians takes you from Trinity College to St. Stephen's Green. You'll pass two venerable department stores: the Irish Brown Thomas and the English Marks & Spencer. Johnson's Court alley leads to the Powerscourt Townhouse Shopping Centre, which tastefully fills a converted Georgian mansion. The huge, glass-covered St. Stephen's Green Shopping Centre and the peaceful green itself mark the top of Grafton Street.

▲St. Stephen's Green

This city park was originally a medieval commons, complete with gory public executions. The park got its start in 1664, when the city leased some of the land as building lots—and each tenant was obligated to plant six trees. Gradually the green was surrounded with fine Georgian buildings. Today (like New York's Central Park) it provides a grassy refuge for Dubliners. At the northwest corner (near the end of Grafton Street) you'll be confronted by a looming marble arch erected to honor British officers killed during the Boer War. Locals nicknamed it "Traitor's Arch," as most Irish sympathized with the underdog Boers.

During the 1916 Easter Rising, a group of passionate rebels—a mishmash of romantic poets, teachers, aristocratic ladies, and slum dwellers—dug trenches in the park to hunker down, believing they were creating fortified positions. They hadn't figured on veteran British troops easily trumping their move by placing snipers atop the Shelbourne Hotel (with a bird's-eye view into the trenches).

On a sunny afternoon, this open space is a wonderful world apart from the big city. When marveling at the elegance of Georgian Dublin, remember that it was the second-most important city in the British Empire in that era.

Little Museum of Dublin

This boisterous little museum facing St. Stephen's Green, just five rooms in a Georgian mansion from 1776, is a creative labor of love. Volunteers have covered its walls with historic bits and pieces of

Dublin history—all donated by locals. This museum also sponsors the City of a Thousand Welcomes Meet a Dubliner program.

Cost and Hours: €8 includes required 30-minute tour, daily 9:30-17:00, Thu until 20:00, tours depart on the hour 10:00-16:00, 15 St. Stephen's Green, tel. 01/661-1000, www.littlemuseum.ie.

Visiting the Museum: Your visit starts with an entertaining 30-minute talk mixing modern Dublin history and pop culture as illustrated in two rooms. Then you're free to wander the remaining rooms (including one on Irish rock 'n' roll for U2 fans and another on local pub culture). Memorabilia range from historic letters written by Irish nationalists Éamon de Valera and Michael Collins to mementos of JFK's 1963 Dublin visit and Muhammad Ali's 1972 fight here.

Dublin Castle and Nearby

If you are in the castle area at lunchtime, consider the recommended Silk Road Café in the Chester Beatty Library (located in the castle gardens; see listing under "Eating in Dublin").

▲Dublin Castle

Built on the spot of the first Viking fortress, this castle was the seat of English rule in Ireland for 700 years. Located where the Poddle and Liffey rivers came to-gether, making a black pool (*dubh linn* in Irish), Dublin Castle was the official residence of the viceroy who implemented the will of the British royalty. In this stirring setting, the Brits handed power over to Michael Collins and the Irish in 1922. Today, it's used for fancy state and charity functions (which may sporadically close it to the public).

Cost and Hours: Visiting the courtyard is free, €10 for one-hour guided tour, €7 to visit on your own (state apartments only); Mon-Sat 10:00-16:45, Sun from 12:00, tours depart every 30 minutes; tickets sold in courtyard under portico opposite clock tower, tel. 01/645-8813, www.dublincastle.ie.

Visiting the Castle: Standing in the courtyard, you can imagine the ugliness of the British-Irish situation. Notice the statue of justice above the gate—pointedly without her blindfold and admiring her sword. As Dubliners say, "There she stands, above her station, with her face to the palace and her arse to the nation."

The fancy interior is viewable on a guided tour, which offers a fairly boring room-by-room walk through the lavish state apartments of this most English of Irish palaces. The tour also includes a look at the foundations of the Norman tower as well as original Viking defenses, and the best remaining chunk of the 13th-century town wall.

▲▲Chester Beatty Library

This library—located in the gardens of Dublin Castle (follow the signs)—is an exquisite, delightfully displayed collection of rare ancient manuscripts and beautifully illustrated books from around the world, plus a few odd curios. These treasures were bequeathed by Alfred Chester Beatty (1875-1968), a rich American mining magnate who traveled widely, collected 66,000 objects assiduously, and retired to Ireland.

Cost and Hours: Free; Mon-Fri 10:00-17:00, Sat from 11:00, Sun from 13:00, closed Mon Nov-Feb; library's Silk Road Café is fine for a light lunch—see listing under "Eating in Dublin"; tel. 01/407-0750, www.cbl.ie.

☉ Self-Guided Tour: Start on the ground floor, with a 10-minute film about Beatty. Then head upstairs to the second floor to see the treasures he left to his adopted country. Note that exhibits often rotate, so they may not be on display in the order outlined here.

Sacred Traditions Gallery: This space is dedicated to sacred texts, illuminated manuscripts, and miniature paintings from around the world. The doors swing open, and you're greeted by a video highlighting a diverse array of religious rites—a Christian wedding, Muslims kneeling for prayer, whirling dervishes, and so on.

• *Tour the floor clockwise, starting with Christian texts on the left side of the room. There you'll find several glass cases containing...*

Ancient Bible Fragments: In the 1930s, Beatty acquired these 1,800-year-old manuscripts, which had recently been unearthed in Egypt. The Indiana Jones-like discovery instantly bumped scholars' knowledge of the early Bible up a notch. There were Old Testament books, New Testament books, and—rarest of all—the Letters of Paul. Written in Greek on papyrus more than a century before previously known documents, these are some of the oldest versions of these texts in existence. Unlike most early Christian texts, the manuscripts were not rolled up in a scroll but bound in a book form called a "codex." On display you may see pages from a third-century Gospel of Luke or the Gospel of John (c. A.D. 150-200). Jesus died around A.D. 33, and his words weren't recorded until decades later. Most early manuscripts date from the fourth century, so these pages are about as close to the source as you can get.

Letters (Epistles) of Paul: The Beatty has 112 pages of Saint Paul's collected letters (A.D. 180-200). Paul, a Roman citizen

(c. A.D. 5-67; see Albrecht Dürer's engraving of the saint), was the apostle most responsible for spreading Christianity beyond Palestine. Originally, Paul reviled Christians. But after a mystical experience, he went on to travel the known world, preaching the Good News in sophisticated Athens and the greatest city in the world, Rome, where he died a martyr to the cause. Along the way, he kept in touch with Christian congregations in cities like Corinth, Ephesus, and Rome with these letters.

Continuing up the left side of the room, you'll find gloriously illustrated medieval Bibles and prayer books, including an intricate, colorful, gold-speckled Book of Hours (1408).

• *Turn the corner into the center of the room, to find the sacred texts of...*

Islam: Muslims believe that the angel Gabriel visited Muhammad (c. 570-632), instructing him to write down his heavenly visions in a book—the Quran. You'll see Qurans with elaborate calligraphy, such as one made in Baghdad in 1001. Nearby are other sacred Islamic texts, some beautifully illustrated, where you may find the rare illuminated manuscript of the "Life of the Prophet" (c. 1595), produced in Istanbul for an Ottoman sultan.

• *On the right side of the room, you enter the world of...*

East Asian Religions: Statues of Gautama Buddha (c. 563-483 B.C.) and Chinese Buddhist scrolls attest to the pervasive influence of this wise man. Buddha was born in India, but his philosophy spread to China, Japan, and Tibet (see the mandalas). Continuing clockwise, you'll reach the writings from India, the land of a million gods—and the cradle of Buddhism, Hinduism, Sikhism, and Jainism.

• *Your visit continues downstairs on the first floor, in the gallery devoted to the...*

Arts of the Book: The focus here is on the many forms a "book" can take—from the earliest clay tablets and papyrus scrolls, to parchment scrolls and bound codexes, to medieval monks' wondrous illustrations, to the advent of printing and bookbinding, to the dawn of the 21st century and the digital age.

• *Tour the floor clockwise. Immediately to the left, find a glass case containing...*

Egyptian and Other Ancient Writings: A hieroglyph-covered papyrus scroll from the Book of the Dead (c. 300 B.C.) depicts a pharaoh on his throne (left) presiding over a soul's judgment in the afterlife. The jackal-headed god Anubis (center-right) holds a scale, weighing the heart of a dead woman to see if it's light enough for her to level up to the next phase of eternity. Nearby (in a free-standing glass case, near the bottom) are a few small cuneiform tablets and cylinder seals from as far back as 2700 B.C. These objects from ancient Sumeria (modern-day Iraq) are older than the pyramids and represent the very birth of writing.

• *Continue up the left side of the room, perusing displays on...*

Printing, Illustrating, and Bookbinding: The printing press with movable type was perfected by Johannes Gutenberg in Germany around 1450. The printed sheets were folded, sewn together, and wrapped in a cover. With the engraving process, beautiful illustrations could also be reproduced on a mass scale. Until the 20th century, it was common for a book buyer to acquire the printed sheets and then select a lavish custom-made cover.

• *Turn the corner to the center of the room.*

Islamic World: These are secular books—science textbooks and poetry—many from the rich Persian culture (modern-day Iran). Some are richly illustrated with elaborate calligraphy. While Islam avoids representations of living things, as you can see, that restriction doesn't apply to nonreligious texts.

• *Continue to the right side of the room.*

Far East: Besides albums and scrolls, you might see eye-catching Japanese woodblock prints, ornate Chinese snuff bottles, rhino-horn cups, and the silk dragon robes of Chinese emperors of the Qing dynasty (1644-1911). The Qianlong Emperor (r. 1736-1795)—a poet and arts patron—welcomed European Jesuits to his court and commissioned a huge collection of books, including some carved from jade.

Dublin City Hall

The first Georgian building in this very Georgian city stands proudly overlooking Dame Street, in front of the gate to Dublin Castle. Built in 1779 as the Royal Exchange (where one changed money), it introduced Ireland to the Georgian style then very popular in Britain. In 1852, the building became the City Hall.

Cost and Hours: Free, Mon-Sat 10:00-17:15, closed Sun, coffee shop, tel. 01/222-2204.

Visiting City Hall: Step inside to feel the prosperity and confidence of Dublin in her 18th-century glory days. Under the grand rotunda, a cycle of heroic paintings tells the city's history in a rare example of Arts and Crafts artwork from 1919. The mosaics on the floor convey such homilies as "Obedience makes the happiest citizenry."

Pay your respects to the 18-foot-tall statue of Daniel O'Connell, the great orator and liberator who, in 1829, won emancipation for Catholics in Ireland from the much-despised Protestants over in London. The body of modern Irish rebel leader Michael Collins lay in state here after his assassination in 1922 (the greeter is happy to give you more information).

Downstairs, don't miss the free "**Story of the Capital**" **exhibit.** It is the best history of Dublin exhibit I have found, traced through artifacts and models as well as excellent video clips, including *The City in Turmoil.*

Dublin's Cathedrals Area

Because of Dublin's English past (particularly Henry VIII's Reformation, and the dissolution of the Catholic monasteries in both Ireland and England in 1539), the city's top two churches are no longer Catholic. Christ Church Cathedral and nearby St. Patrick's Cathedral are both Church of Ireland (Anglican). In the late 19th century, the cathedrals underwent extensive restoration. The rich Guinness brewery family forked out the dough to try to make St. Patrick's Cathedral outshine Christ Church—whose patrons were the equally rich, rival Jameson family of distillery fame.

Christ Church Cathedral

Occupying the same site as the first wooden church built on this spot by King Sitric in late Viking times (c. 1030), the present structure is a mix of periods: Norman and Gothic, but mostly Victorian Neo-Gothic from the late 19th century.

Cost and Hours: €6.50 includes downstairs crypt exhibition, €14.50 combo-ticket includes Dublinia (described next); Mon-Sat 9:30-17:00, Sun 12:00-14:30; €4 guided tours Mon-Fri at 11:00, 12:00, 14:00, and 15:00; tel. 01/677-8099, www.christchurchdublin.ie.

Church Services and Evensong: There's a full Anglican service Sun at 11:00, and the public is welcome to a 45-minute evensong service, sung by the esteemed Christ Church choir (Wed-Thu at 18:00, Sun at 15:30).

Visiting the Cathedral: The interior is Victorian, from the 1870s. Highlights are the finely carved wooden quire (with the grand bishop's seat) and the tomb of Strongbow, the Norman warlord who helped conquer Ireland, leading to centuries of British domination. (While he was buried here in 1176, this stone is a 14th-century replacement.) From the south transept, stairs lead down into the crypt—considered the oldest structure in town (open to the public). Running the entire length of the church (with a forest of stout supporting columns), it's filled with historic odds and ends (and a WC).

▲Dublinia

This exhibit, which highlights Dublin's Viking and medieval past, is a hit with youngsters (but meaty enough for adults as well).

Cost and Hours: €9.50, €14.50 combo-ticket includes Christ Church Cathedral; daily 10:00-18:30, Oct-Feb until 17:30, last entry one hour before closing; top-floor coffee shop, across from Christ Church Cathedral, tel. 01/679-4611, www.dublinia.ie.

Visiting the Exhibits: The displays are laid out on three floors.

The ground floor focuses on Viking Dublin, explaining life aboard a Viking ship and inside a Viking house. Viking traders introduced urban life and commerce to Ireland—but kids will be most interested in gawking at their gory weaponry.

The next floor up reveals Dublin's day-to-day life in medieval times, from chivalrous knights and damsels in town fairs to the brutal ravages of the plague. Like so much of Europe at that time (1347-1349), Ireland lost one-third of its population to the Black Death. The huge scale model of medieval Dublin is especially well done. The top floor's "History Hunters" section is devoted to how the puzzles of modern archaeology and science shed light on Dublin's history. From this floor, you can climb a couple of flights of stairs into the tower for so-so views of Dublin, or exit across an enclosed stone bridge to adjacent Christ Church Cathedral.

St. Patrick's Cathedral

This Anglican cathedral is a thoughtful learning experience as well as a living church. The first church here was Catholic, supposedly built on the site where St. Patrick baptized local pagan converts. While the core of the Gothic structure you see today was built in the 13th century, most of today's stonework is 19th century. After the Reformation, it passed into the hands of the Anglican Church. A century later, Oliver Cromwell's puritanical Calvinist troops—who considered the Anglicans to be little more than Catholics without a pope—stabled their horses here as a sign of disrespect.

Cost and Hours: €6.50 donation to church; Mon-Fri 9:30-17:00, Sat-Sun 9:00-18:00—but on Sun it's closed 10:30-12:30 and 14:30-16:30, last entry one hour before closing; at the intersection of Patrick Street and Upper Kevin Street, www.stpatrickscathedral.ie.

Tours: Free guided tours are given several times a day in summer; check website for schedule but typically at 10:30, 11:30, 14:30, 15:00, and 15:30.

Evensong: You'll get chills listening to the local "choir of angels" Mon-Fri at 17:30 and Sun at 15:15.

Visiting the Cathedral: The inside feels like an Irish Westminster Abbey, with venerable tombs and memorials to great Irish figures everywhere. The fine Victorian glass is from a Guinness-funded restoration in the 1870s. The regimental flags of the British army hang from the ceiling, colors slowly fading, in remembrance of soldiers lost. The north transept is dedicated to music (they claim Handel's *Messiah* was first performed here in 1742). The south transept is "The Discovery Space," a delightful learning center with thousand-year-old gravestones and free brass rubbing.

Jonathan Swift (author of *Gulliver's Travels*) was dean of the cathedral from 1713 to 1745. His grave and death mask are located

DUBLIN

near the front door (on the right side of the nave), where his cutting, self-penned epitaph reads: "He lies where furious indignation can no longer rend his heart."

▲▲Temple Bar

This much-promoted area—with shops, cafés, theaters, galleries, pubs with live music, and restaurants—feels like the heart of the old city. It's Dublin's touristy "Left Bank," on the south shore of the river, filling the cobbled streets between Dame Street and the River Liffey.

Three hundred years ago, this was the city waterfront, where tall sailing ships offloaded their goods (a "bar" was a loading dock along the river, and the Temples were a dominant merchant family). Eventually, the city grew eastward, filling in tidal mudflats, to create the docklands of modern Dublin. Once a thriving Georgian center of craftsmen and merchants, this neighborhood fell on hard times in the 20th century. Ensuing low rents attracted students and artists, giving the area a bohemian flair. With government tax incentives and lots of development money, the Temple Bar district has now become a thriving entertainment (and beer-drinking) hot spot.

Sights and Activities in Temple Bar: Temple Bar Square, just off Temple Bar Street (near Ha' Penny Bridge), is the epicenter of activity. It hosts free street theater and a **Saturday book market.** On busy weekends, people-watching here is a contact sport (and pickpocketing is not).

Irish music fans find great CDs at humble **Claddagh Records** (Cecilia Street, just around the corner from Luigi Malone's, Mon-Sat 11:00-17:30, closed Sun, tel. 01/677-0262). Unlike big, glitzy chain stores, this is a little hole-in-the-wall shop staffed by informed folks who love turning visitors on to Irish tunes. Grab a couple of CDs for your drive through the Irish countryside.

Farther west and somewhat hidden is Meeting House Square, with a lively **organic-produce market** (Sat 10:00-18:00). Bordering the square is the **Irish Film Institute** (main entry on Eustace Street), which shows a variety of art-house flicks. A bohemian crowd relaxes in its bar/café, awaiting the next film (6 Eustace Street, box office daily 13:30-21:00, tel. 01/679-5744, www.irishfilm.ie).

Less commercial plays can be seen nearby at **Smock Alley Theatre,** with seating surrounding a tiny stage, in a space on the site of the city's first custom-built theater from 1662.

Eating in and near Temple Bar: I've listed my recommendations later in this chapter (see "Eating in Dublin," later). But if you want to wander on your own without following particular recom-mendations, venture down a few side lanes off the main drag to see what looks good. If the rowdy Temple Bar scene gets to be too much, cross over to the north bank of the River Liffey on the Millennium Pedestrian Bridge (next bridge west of the Ha' Penny Bridge), where you'll find a mellower, more cosmopolitan choice of restaurants with outdoor seating in the Millennium Walk district.

Nighttime Rowdiness: Temple Bar can be an absolute spectacle in the evening, when it bursts with revelers. The noise, pushy crowds and inflated prices have driven most Dubliners away. But even if you're just gawking, don't miss the opportunity to wander through this human circus. It's craziest on summer weekend nights, holidays, and nights after big sporting events let out. Women in funky hats, part of loud "hen" (bachelorette) parties, promenade down the main drag as drunken dudes shout from pub doorways to get their attention. You're bound to meet some characters and might even have to step around some "sidewalk pizza."

NORTH OF THE RIVER LIFFEY

O'Connell Street and the historic core north of the river is covered by the self-guided walk on page 18. After you're oriented with the walk, consider the following sights.

▲▲Epic: The Irish Emigration Museum

Telling the story of the Irish diaspora, this museum celebrates how this little island has had an oversized impact on the world. While the museum has no actual artifacts, this is an entertaining and educational experience.

Cost and Hours: €14, daily 10:00-18:45, last entry at 17:00, one-hour tours at 11:00 and 14:00, in the CHQ building on Custom House Quay (at the modern pedestrian bridge a few steps from the famine statues along the riverfront), tel. 01/906-0861, www.epicchq.com.

Visiting the Museum: The museum fills the wine vaults in the basement of an iron-framed warehouse from the 1820s (where the customs house stood on the River Liffey). Its 20 themed galleries take an interactive, high-tech approach to explain the forces that propelled so many Irish around the globe. Featured illustrious emigrants include labor agitator Mother Jones, Caribbean pirate Anne Bonny, Australian bush bandit Ned Kelly, and musical Chicago police chief Francis O'Neill. Historic photos of filthy tenements and early films of bustling urban scenes document the plight of the common Irish emigrant. And all along you celebrate Irish heritage in music, literature, sports, and more.

Genealogy Help: Upstairs from the museum, the **Irish Family History Centre** can help you research your Celtic roots (€10 to access research stations, €40 for 30-minute consultation, daily 10:00-17:00, tel. 01/905-9216, www.irishfamilyhistorycentre.com).

Nearby: Today the modern **food court** in the CHQ building serves the glassy office towers that now energize what, 30 years ago, was an urban wasteland. A modern **pedestrian bridge**—shaped like an old Irish harp and designed by Santiago Calatrava—leads to Dublin's strikingly contemporary convention center.

Before leaving the riverside area, cross Customs House Quay (the main road) and wander 50 yards up the River Liffey toward the city to contemplate the skeletal sculptures of the city's evocative **Famine Memorial.** A few steps in the opposite direction, downriver, you'll spot the masts of the Jeanie Johnston Tall Ship and Famine Museum (see next). A visit here ties in well with the area's emigration theme.

▲Jeanie Johnston Tall Ship and Famine Museum

Docked on the River Liffey, this seagoing sailing ship is a replica of a legendary Irish "famine ship." The original *Jeanie Johnston* embarked on 16 eight-week transatlantic crossings, carrying more than 2,500 Irish emigrants (about 200 per voyage) to their new lives in America and Canada in the decade after the Great Potato Famine of the 1840s. While many barely seaworthy hulks were known as "coffin ships," the people who boarded the *Jeanie Johnston* were lucky: The ship was Irish owned and crewed, with a humanitarian captain and even a doctor on board, and not one life was lost. Your tour guide will introduce you to the ship's main characters and help illuminate day-to-day life aboard a cramped tall ship 160 years ago.

Note that, because this ship makes goodwill voyages to Atlantic ports, it may be away during your visit—check ahead.

Cost and Hours: €10, visits by 50-minute tour only, easy to book slot in advance online; daily April-Sept 10:00-16:00, Oct-March 11:00-15:00, tours depart on the hour (but no tours at 13:00); on the north bank of the Liffey just east of Sean O'Casey Bridge, tel. 01/473-0111, www.jeaniejohnston.ie.

▲Dublin Writers Museum

No other country so small has produced such a wealth of literature. As interesting to those who are fans of Irish literature as it is boring to those who aren't, this three-room museum features the lives and works of Dublin's great writers. It's a low-tech museum, where you read informative plaques while perusing display cases with minor memorabilia—a document signed by Jonathan Swift, a photo of Oscar Wilde reclining thoughtfully, an early edition of Bram Stoker's *Dracula*, a George Bernard Shaw playbill, a not-so-famous author's tuxedo, or a newspaper from Easter 1916 announcing "Two More Executions Today." If unassuming attractions like that stir your blood—or if you simply want a manageable introduction to Irish lit—it's worth a visit.

Cost and Hours: €7.50, includes helpful 45-minute audioguide; Mon-Sat 9:45-17:00, Sun from 11:00; 18 Parnell Square North, tel. 01/872-2077, www.writersmuseum.com.

Visiting the Museum: The collection is chronological. While you'll follow the audioguide, here are some highlights:

Room 1 starts with Irish literature's deep roots in the roving, harp-playing bards of medieval times. By telling stories in the native language, they helped unify the island's culture. But "literature" came only with the arrival of the English language. **Jonathan Swift** (1667-1745)—Ireland's first great writer—was born in Dublin and served as dean of St. Patrick's Cathedral, though he spent much of his life in London. His stinging satire of societal hypocrisy set the tone of rebellion found in much Irish literature. The theater has been another longstanding Irish specialty, starting with the 18th-century playwright Oliver Goldsmith. In the 1890s, sophisticated Dublin (and Trinity College) was a cradle for great writers who ultimately found their fortunes in England: the playwright/poet/wit Oscar Wilde, Bram Stoker (who married Wilde's girlfriend), and the big-idea playwright George Bernard Shaw. Poet **W. B. Yeats** stayed home, cultivating Irish folklore at soirees (hosted by the literary patron Lady Augusta Gregory).

Room 2 continues into the 20th century with Yeats' **Abbey Theatre,** the scene of premieres by great Irish playwrights (including Yeats, Shaw, and Wilde), and an important force in the developing sense of Irish national identity in the early part of the century. Dublin was also a breeding ground for bold new ideas, producing Modernist writers Samuel *(Waiting for Godot)* Beckett and James Joyce (a center devoted to him is described next). As the 20th century progressed, writers like Sean O'Casey, Brendan Behan, Seamus Heaney, John B. Keane, and Brian Friel kept Dublin at the forefront of modern theater.

Finish your visit by going **upstairs** to see an elegant Georgian library with portraits, busts, and temporary exhibits on Irish literature.

James Joyce Centre

Only aficionados of James Joyce's work will want to visit this micromuseum.

Cost and Hours: €5, Mon-Sat 10:00-17:00, Sun from 12:00,

DUBLIN

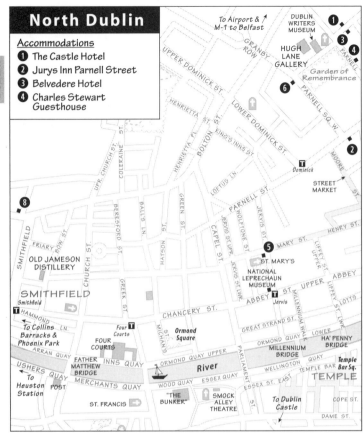

North Dublin

Accommodations
1. The Castle Hotel
2. Jurys Inn Parnell Street
3. Belvedere Hotel
4. Charles Stewart Guesthouse

closed Mon Oct-March, two blocks east of the Dublin Writers Museum at 35 North Great George's Street, tel. 01/878-8547, www.jamesjoyce.ie. The center offers walking tours of Joyce sights several times a week.

Background: Born and raised in Dublin, James Joyce (1882-1941) wrote in great detail about his hometown, and mined the local dialect for his pitch-perfect dialogue. His best-known work, *Ulysses,* chronicles one day (June 16, 1904) in the life of the fictional Leopold Bloom as he wanders through the underside of Dublin. Joyce himself left Dublin (on June 17, 1904) for Paris and lived away from the city for most of his life. He never took up the cause of Irish nationalism and rarely delved into Irish mythology. He instead wrote with a new Modernist focus on linguistic invention and social frankness.

Visiting the Center: Your visit begins (top floor) with videos on Joyce's life and his enormous influence on subsequent writers. Next, a touchscreen display traces Bloom's Dublin Odyssey. Pho-

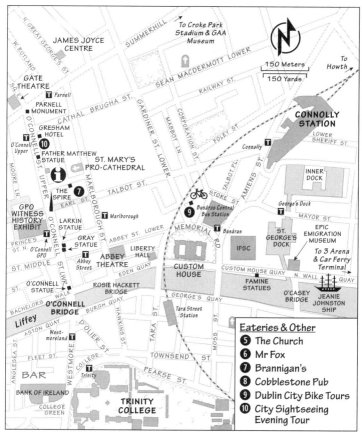

Eateries & Other
- **5** The Church
- **6** Mr Fox
- **7** Brannigan's
- **8** Cobblestone Pub
- **9** Dublin City Bike Tours
- **10** City Sightseeing Evening Tour

tos of Joyce and quotes from his books decorate the walls. A re-creation of a messy, cramped study evokes Joyce's struggles through poverty and criticism as he forged his own path. Down one flight, see portraits of Joyce and his wife and muse, Nora Barnacle. (The first time they, um, went on a date was June 16, 1904. Joyce later set the events depicted in his masterpiece, *Ulysses*, on that date, which is commemorated annually as Bloomsday in honor of Leopold Bloom.) On the ground floor, a film version of one of Joyce's short stories, *The Dead*, plays eternally. In a tiny back courtyard, you can see the original door from 7 Eccles Street, the address of Leopold Bloom.

▲Hugh Lane Gallery

This stimulating and well-described exhibit of art from the 1870s onward includes a sampling of Impressionist masterpieces from the gallery's founding collection, once owned by Sir Hugh Lane, an Irish art dealer. Genteel and bite-sized, the museum is particularly

Dublin's Literary Life

Dublin in the 1700s, grown rich from a lucrative cloth trade, was one of Europe's most cultured and sophisticated cities.

The buildings were decorated in the Georgian style still visible today, and the city's Protestant elite shuttled between here and London, bridging the Anglo-Irish cultural gap. Jonathan Swift (1667-1745) was the era's greatest Anglo-Irish writer—a brilliant satirist and author of *Gulliver's Travels*. He was also dean of St. Patrick's Cathedral (1713-1745) and one of the city's eminent citizens.

Around the turn of the 20th century, Dublin produced some of the world's great modern writers. Bram Stoker (1847-1912) was creator of *Dracula*. Oscar Wilde (1854-1900) penned *The Picture of Dorian Gray* and a clutch of fine plays. George Bernard Shaw (1856-1950) wrote *Pygmalion*, *Major Barbara*, *Man and Superman*, and a host of other dramas. William Butler Yeats (1865-1939) was a prolific poet and playwright on Irish themes. And James Joyce (1882-1941) whipped up a masterpiece called *Ulysses*. For more on Irish literature, see page 46.

To dip your toe into the occasionally unfathomable depths of classic Irish lit, drop by the tiny **Sweny's Pharmacy** for one of its daily readings from *Ulysses*. This shrine for devotees of Joyce is a time capsule, looking just as the writer described it in his novel more than a hundred years ago. The text is passed around for all to read a section aloud, and even if you don't understand its obscure local references, appreciate the rhythm of its stream-of-consciousness verbal flow...and buy a bar of lemon soap on your way out (daily, usually at 13:00, check schedule at www.sweny.ie, sometimes read in other languages...might make it easier to figure out, 1 Lincoln Place between Trinity College and Merrion Square).

worth a visit for a well-known Monet painting, an exhibit on modern artist Francis Bacon, and a few select paintings by Irish artists.

Cost and Hours: Free, Tue-Thu 10:00-18:00, Fri-Sat until 17:00, Sun 11:00-17:00, closed Mon, in the Dublin City Gallery on Parnell Square North, tel. 01/222-5550, www.hughlane.ie.

Visiting the Gallery: Head to Room 1, where you'll find **Monet's *Waterloo Bridge*** (1900). On a visit to London, the once-bohemian, now-famous Impressionist Claude Monet checked into Room 618 of the Savoy Hotel and set to work painting Waterloo Bridge at different times of day and in various weather conditions.

This painting is just one of 41 versions of the scene. Monet—the master of capturing hazy, filtered light—loved London for its fog. With the Thames in the foreground, the bridge in the middle, and belching smokestacks in the distance, Monet had three different layers of atmospheric depth to explore.

In 1905, Sir Hugh bought Monet's *Waterloo Bridge* as part of his mission to bring modern art to the British Isles and provincial Dublin. Unfortunately, Sir Hugh went down on the *Lusitania* in 1915 and didn't see this gallery open. To see a depiction of dapper Sir Hugh—by the American society portraitist John Singer Sargent—find the room to the right of Room 3.

Francis Bacon Studio: Although he spent most of his life in London, Francis Bacon (1909-1992) was born in Dublin and raised nearby. After his death, his entire London studio was reconstructed here, just as the artist had left it.

After a wandering youth of odd jobs and petty crime, Bacon took up painting in his late thirties. He jumped onto the art stage in 1945 with his bleak canvases of twisted, deformed, screaming-mouthed men caged in barren landscapes—which hauntingly captured the mood of post-WWII Europe. He would become Britain's premier painter, but he continued to live simply. He stayed in his small, cramped flat with an even smaller studio (this one) for his entire life. Here he painted his famous series of "Heads"—portraits of his friends, especially of his life partner, George Dyer.

The place is a mess—empty paint cans, slashed canvases, books, photos, and newspapers everywhere—leaving only enough space for Bacon to set up his canvas in the middle of it all and paint. As trashed as the studio is, it reflects Bacon's belief that "chaos breeds energy."

Spend 10 minutes with the 1985 filmed interview of Bacon, which was conducted in the studio. He speaks articulately about his work and reminisces about his down-and-out days. In nearby rooms are photos of Bacon, a few unfinished works, and display cases of personal items, such as his coffee-table book on Velázquez, the Old Master who inspired Bacon's famous portrait of a screaming pope.

▲▲GPO Witness History Exhibit

During the Easter Rising in 1916, Irish nationalists took over various buildings in Dublin, including the General Post Office (GPO), which became the rebel headquarters. Initial euphoria led to chaotic street battles and ended with the grim realization among the insurgents that surrender was the best option—trusting that their martyrdom would inspire the country to rise more effectively. This engaging permanent exhibit—in the working GPO—explores that pivotal Easter Week.

Cost and Hours: €12, Mon-Fri 9:00-17:30, Thu until 19:00 in July-Aug, Sat-Sun 10:00-17:30 year-round, last entry one hour before closing, audioguide-€1, tel. 01/872-1916, www.gpowitnesshistory.ie.

Background: A sideshow for European nations preoccupied with World War I, the Easter Rising was critical to Irish nationalists. Almost every Irish generation for the preceding 125 years had launched doomed insurrections. But this one had a lasting effect, although it may not have seemed so in its immediate wake—a couple of weeks later, the patriot leaders who held their ground at the GPO were executed in Kilmainham Gaol. Public sympathies shifted seismically. From this point on, after seven centuries of dominance, the British were on a slippery slope leading to the eventual granting of independence to its nearest and oldest colony.

Visiting the Exhibit: You'll find the exhibit, with many interesting artifacts, on the right as you enter the building. It features a fairly balanced view of the rebellion, including the less popular realities (like the lack of widespread support at the beginning of the movement and the civilians who died in the crossfire). Don't miss the excellent 15-minute wide-screen depiction of events (called "The Rising") in the tiny theater. An interactive map of Dublin zooms in and out of various neighborhoods, tracking the week's confrontations, with actors dramatizing the events and conversations that shaped the conflict. In video presentations, historians give their take on how the rebellion affected Irish history.

National Leprechaun Museum

This corny, low-tech attraction is fine for kids and lighthearted adults. An uninhibited guide leads the group on a 45-minute meander through Irish mythology. You'll visit a wishing well, a giant's living room, and a fairy fort, listening to tales that will enchant your wee ones.

Cost and Hours: €14, daily 10:00-18:30, last entry one hour before closing, a block north of the River Liffey on Abbey Street across from Jervis LUAS stop, tel. 01/873-3899, www.leprechaunmuseum.ie.

Evening Visits: For adults only, a one-hour, interactive "This Dark Land" storytelling performance explores the macabre side of Irish folklore (€16, May-Sept Fri-Sat at 19:30 and 20:30).

Old Jameson Distillery

Whiskey fans enjoy visiting the old distillery. You get a 40-minute tour and a free shot in the pub. Unfortunately, the "distillery" feels corporate, overpriced, and put together for tourists. The Bushmills tour in Northern Ireland (in a working factory) and the Midleton

From Famine to Revolution

After the Great Potato Famine (1845-1849), destitute rural Irish moved to the city in droves, seeking work and causing a housing shortage. Unscrupulous landlords came up with a solution: Subdivide the city's once-grand mansions, vacated when gentry moved to London after the 1801 Act of Union. The mansions' tiny rooms could then be crammed with poor renters. Dublin became one of the most densely populated cities in Europe—one of every three Dubliners lived in a slum. On Henrietta Street, once a wealthy Dublin address, these new tenements bulged with humanity. According to the 1911 census, one district counted 835 people living in 15 houses (many with a single outhouse in back or a communal chamber pot in the room). In cramped, putrid quarters like this, tuberculosis was rampant, and infant mortality skyrocketed.

Those who could get work tenaciously clung to their precious jobs. The terrible working conditions prompted many to join trade unions. A 1913 strike and employer lockout, known as the "Dublin Lockout," lasted for seven months. The picket lines were brutally put down by police in the pocket of rich businessmen, led by newspaper owner and hotel magnate William Murphy. In response, James Larkin and James Connolly formed the Irish Citizen Army, a socialist militia to protect the poor trade unionists.

Murphy eventually broke the unions. Larkin headed for the US to organize workers there. During World War I, he praised the rise of the Soviet Union and later was persecuted during the postwar "Red Scare" (even doing time in Sing Sing prison for advocating "unlawful means" to overthrow the US government). Meanwhile, Connolly stayed in Ireland and brought the Irish Citizen Army into the 1916 Easter Rising as an integral part of the rebel forces. During the uprising, he slyly had a rebel flag flown over Murphy's prized hotel on O'Connell Street. The uninformed British artillery battalions took the bait and pulverized it.

Connolly was the last of the rebel leaders executed in Dublin in 1916. Unable to stand in front of the firing squad in Kilmainham Gaol (his gangrenous ankle had been shattered by a bullet while he was defending the General Post Office), Connolly was tied to a chair and shot sitting down. Of the 16 rebel executions, Connolly's was most credited with turning Irish public opinion in favor of the rebel martyrs (due to his devoted following among poor tenement dwellers).

Today you'll find heroic Dublin statues to honor both men. James Larkin, arms outstretched, is in front of the post office on O'Connell Street. James Connolly is on Beresford Place, behind the Customs House.

tour near Cork (in the huge original factory) are better experiences. If you do take this tour, volunteer energetically when offered the chance: This will get you a coveted seat at the whiskey taste-test table at the tour's end.

Cost and Hours: €20, Mon-Sat 9:30-18:00, Sun from 10:00, last tour at 17:15, late tours possible in summer; Bow Street, tel. 01/807-2355, www.jamesonwhiskey.com.

Nearby: The neighborhood called **Smithfield** was on the fast track to gentrification prior to the 2008-2009 economic crash. Today, it's getting back on its feet and is home to both the Old Jameson Distillery and Dublin's most authentic traditional-music pub. Both are on the long Smithfield Square, two blocks northwest of the Four Courts—the Supreme Court building. The **Fresh Market,** near the top of the square, is a handy grocery stop for urban picnic fixings (daily until 22:00).

OUTER DUBLIN

The Kilmainham Gaol (GAY-ol) and the Guinness Storehouse are located west of the old center and can be linked by a 20-minute walk, a five-minute taxi ride, or public bus #40 or #13. (To ride the bus from the jail to the Guinness Storehouse, leave the prison and take three rights—crossing no streets—to reach the bus stop.) Another option is to take a hop-on, hop-off bus, which stops at both sights.

▲▲▲Kilmainham Gaol

Opened in 1796 as Dublin's county jail and a debtors' prison, Kilmainham was considered a model in its day. In reality, this jail was frequently used by the British as a political prison. Many of those who fought for Irish independence were held or executed here, including leaders of the rebellions of 1798, 1803, 1848, 1867, and 1916. National heroes Robert Emmett and Charles Stewart Parnell each did time here. The last prisoner to be held in the jail  was Éamon de Valera, who later became president of Ireland. He was released on July 16, 1924, the day Kilmainham was finally shut down. The buildings, virtually in ruins, were restored in the 1960s. Today, it's a shrine to the Nathan Hales of Ireland.

Cost and Hours: €8 includes guided one-hour jail tour and unguided museum visit; daily June-Aug 9:00-18:45, last tour at 17:30; Sept-May 9:30-17:30, last tour at 16:15; tours run 2/hour, tel. 01/453-5984, www.kilmainhamgaolmuseum.ie.

Advance Tickets: In the busy season, be sure to book online a few days before your visit to guarantee a spot on a tour, as walk-up spots go quickly. (You can't book by phone, but you can call to see if tours have seats open.) If you need to wait for your tour departure, visit the museum first (or head across the street and through the park to visit the free Irish Museum of Modern Art—15 minutes on foot).

Getting There: Hop-on, hop-off buses stop here, or take bus #69 or #70 from Aston Quay or #13 or #40 from O'Connell Street or College Green—confirm with driver.

Visiting the Jail: Start your visit with a one-hour guided tour (includes 15-minute prison-history slide show in the prison chapel). It's touching to tour the cells and places of execution—hearing tales of oppressive colonialism and heroic patriotism—alongside Irish schoolkids who know these names well. The museum has an excellent exhibit on Victorian prison life and Ireland's fight for independence.

Don't miss the dimly lit "Last Words 1916" hall upstairs, which displays the stirring final letters that patriots sent to loved ones hours before facing the firing squad. Regrettably, transcriptions of the letters are not posted, denying visitors a better understanding of the passion and patriotism of Ireland's greatest in their own last words—a lost opportunity for Americans not realizing that there are other Nathan Hales in this world who wish they had more than one life to give for their country. (Fortunately, the little bookshop for budding patriots carries the inspirational *Last Words* book.)

▲Guinness Storehouse

A visit to the Guinness Storehouse is, for many, a pilgrimage. Arthur Guinness began brewing the renowned stout here in 1759, and by 1868 it was the biggest brewery in the world. Today, the sprawling complex fills several city blocks (64 acres busy brewing 1.5 million pints a day).

Visitors (1.5 million annually) are welcomed to the towering storehouse, where the vibe is glitzy entertainment. Don't look for conveyor belts of beer bottles being stamped with bottle caps, or displays of historic artifacts. Rather than a brewery tour, this is a Disneyland for beer lovers—huge crowds, high decibel music, and dreamy TV beer ads on big screens.

Cost and Hours: €20, includes a €5 pint; daily 9:30-19:00, July-Aug until 20:00, last entry two hours before closing, last

The Famous Record-Breaking Records Book

Look up "beer" in the *Guinness World Records*, and you'll discover that the record for removing beer bottle caps with one's teeth is 68 in one minute. But aside from listing records for amazing—or amazingly stupid—feats, this famous record book has a more subtle connection with beer.

In 1951, while hunting in Ireland's County Wexford, Sir Hugh Beaver, then the managing director at Guinness Breweries, got into a debate with his companions over which was the fastest game bird in Europe: the golden plover or the red grouse. That night at his estate, after scouring countless reference books, they were disappointed not to find a definitive answer.

Beaver realized that similar questions were likely being debated nightly across pubs in Ireland and Britain. So he hired a fact-finding team in London to compile a book of answers to various questions. In 1955, the *Guinness Book of Records* (later renamed *Guinness World Records*) was published. By Christmas, it topped the British bestseller list.

In the beginning, entries mostly focused on natural phenomena and animal oddities, but grew to include a wide variety of extreme human achievements.

The iconic books are now available in more than 100 countries and 26 languages, with more than 3.5 million copies sold annually. As the bestselling copyrighted book of all time, it even earns a record-breaking entry within its own pages.

beer served 45 minutes before closing; tel. 01/408-4800, www. guinness-storehouse.com.

Getting There: Ride the hop-on, hop-off bus (your HOHO ticket gives you a €1 discount here), or take bus #13, #40, or #123 from Dame Street and O'Connell Street. Enter the brewery on Bellevue Street.

Crowd Control: Lines can be horrible at peak times, both outside and at various stops within the brewery. To avoid the worst of it, start early and consider an online booking (tickets discounted 20 percent between 9:30 and 10:45).

Visiting the Brewery: The exhibit fills the old fermentation plant, used from 1902 through 1988, which reopened in 2000 as a huge shrine to the Guinness tradition. Step into the middle of the ground floor and look up. A tall, beer-glass-shaped glass atrium—14 million pints big (that's about 10 days' production)—soars upward past four floors of exhibitions and cafés to the skylight. Then look down at Arthur's original 9,000-year lease, enshrined under Plexiglas in the floor. At £45 per year, it was quite a bargain.

As you escalate ever higher, you'll notice that each floor has a theme. The first floor is dedicated to cooperage—the making of wooden barrels (with 1954 film clips showing master kegmakers working at their now virtually extinct trade); the second floor has the tasting rooms (described below); the third floor features advertising and a theater with classic TV ads; the fourth floor is where you can pull your own beer (at the Academy); and the fifth floor has Arthur's Bar. The top floor is the Gravity Bar, providing visitors with a commanding 360-degree view of Dublin—with vistas all the way to the sea—and an included pint of the beloved stout.

The tasting rooms (on level 2) provide a fun detour. In the "white room" you're introduced to using your five senses to appreciate the perfect porter. Then, in the "velvet chamber," you're taught how to taste it from a leprechaun-sized beer glass.

Claiming Your Beer: Your admission includes a ticket for a beer, which you can claim on one of three levels. On level 4, you can pull your own pint (and then drink it). On level 5, at Arthur's Bar, you can choose among extra stout (4.2%, carbonated), Dublin Porter (3.8%, 1796 recipe), West Indies Porter (6%, toffee flavor, 1801 recipe), Hop House 13 (4.1%, a hoppy lager), and Black Velvet (half and half sparkling wine and Guinness). On the top floor (where there's the most energy and fun), drinks are limited to the basic stout or soft drinks.

▲National Museum: Decorative Arts and History

This branch of the National Museum, which occupies the huge, 18th-century stone Collins Barracks in west Dublin, displays Irish dress, furniture, weapons, silver, and other domestic baubles from the past 700 years. History buffs will linger longest in the "Soldiers & Chiefs" exhibit, which covers the Irish at war both at home and abroad since 1500 (including the American Civil War). The sober finale is the "Proclaiming the Republic" room, offering Ireland's best coverage of the painful birth of this nation. Guns, flags, and personal letters help illustrate the 1916 Easter Rising, the War of Independence against Britain, and Ireland's civil war. Croppies Acre, the large park between the museum and the river, was the site of Dublin's largest soup kitchen during the Great Potato Famine in 1845-1849.

Cost and Hours: Free, Tue-Sat 10:00-17:00, Sun from 14:00, closed Mon, good café; on north side of the River Liffey in Collins Barracks on Benburb Street, roughly across the river from Guinness Storehouse, LUAS red line: Museum stop; tel. 01/677-7444, www.museum.ie.

▲Gaelic Athletic Association Museum

The GAA was founded in 1884 as an expression of an Irish cultural awakening. It was created to foster the development of Gaelic sports, specifically Gaelic football and hurling, and to exclude English sports such as cricket and rugby. The GAA played an important part in the fight for independence. This museum, at 82,000-seat Croke Park Stadium in northeast Dublin, offers a high-tech, interactive introduction to Ireland's favorite games. Relive the greatest moments in hurling and Irish-football history. Then get involved: Pick up a stick and try hurling, kick a football, and test your speed and balance. A 15-minute film (played on request) gives you a "Sunday at the stadium" experience.

Cost and Hours: €7, Mon-Sat 9:30-17:00, June-Aug until 18:00, Sun 10:30-17:00 year-round—except on game Sundays, when the museum is open to ticket holders only; café, located under the stands at Croke Park Stadium, enter from St. Joseph's Avenue off Clonliffe Road, tel. 01/819-2323, www.crokepark.ie/gaa-museum.

Tours: The €14, one-hour museum-plus-stadium-tour option (daily at 11:00, 13:00, and 15:00) is worth it only for rabid fans who want a glimpse of the huge stadium and locker rooms. The €20 rooftop tour offers views 17 stories above the field from lofty catwalks (Mon-Fri at 11:30 and 14:30, Sat-Sun hourly from 10:30 to 14:30; fewer tours Oct-April).

Hurling or Gaelic Football at Croke Park Stadium

Actually seeing a match here, surrounded by incredibly spirited Irish fans, is a fun experience. Hurling is fast and rough: like air-

borne hockey with no injury time-outs. Gaelic football resembles a rugged form of soccer; you can carry the ball, but must bounce or kick it every three steps. Matches are held most Saturday or Sunday afternoons in summer (May-Aug), culminating in the hugely popular all-Ireland finals on Sunday afternoons in September. Tickets are available at the stadium except during the finals. Choose a county to support, buy their colors to wear or wave, scream yourself hoarse, and you'll be a temporary local.

Cost and Hours: €20-55, box office open Mon-Fri 9:30-13:00 & 14:15-17:30, www.gaa.ie.

Getting There: Croke Park is located on the north bank of the Royal Canal, about 10 blocks north of the Connolly train station. It can be reached by bus #40 or #41, or by taxi.

Glasnevin Cemetery Museum

This is the final resting place for Ireland's most passionate patriots, writers, politicians, and assorted personalities. What Père Lachaise

Ireland's Gaelic Athletic Association

The GAA has long been a powerhouse in Ireland. Ireland's national pastimes of Gaelic football and hurling pack stadiums all over the country. When you consider that 82,000 people—paying about €25 each—stuff Dublin's Croke Park Stadium and that all the athletes are strictly amateur, you might wonder, "Where does all the money go?"

Ireland has a long tradition of using the revenue generated by these huge events to promote Gaelic athletics and Gaelic cultural events throughout the country in a grassroots and neighborhood way. So, while the players (many of whom are schoolteachers whose jobs allow for evenings and summers free) participate only for the glory of their various counties, the money generated is funding children's leagues, school coaches, small-town athletic facilities, and traditional arts, music, and dance—as well as the building and maintenance of giant stadiums such as Croke Park.

In Ireland, sports have a deep emotional connection as a heartfelt expression of Irish identity. There was a time when membership in the GAA was denied to anyone who also attended "foreign games," defined as rugby, soccer, or cricket. If the Brits played it, it was viewed as cultural poison. So intractable was this rule that in 1938, Douglas Hyde (then president of Ireland) was kicked out of the GAA for attending an international soccer match. (The rule was abolished in 1971 with the advent of TV sports.)

In 1921, during the War of Independence, IRA leader Michael Collins orchestrated the simultaneous assassination of a dozen British intelligence agents around Dublin in a single morning. The same day, the Black and Tans retaliated. These grizzled British WWI veterans, clad in black police coats and tan surplus army pants, had been sent to Ireland to stamp out the rebels. Knowing Croke Park would be full of Irish Nationalists, they entered the packed stadium during a Gaelic football match and fired into the stands, killing 13 spectators as well as a Tipperary player.

Today Croke Park's "Hill 16" grandstands are built on rubble dumped here after the 1916 Rising; it's literally sacred ground. And the Hogan stands are named after the murdered player from Tipperary. Queen Elizabeth II visited the stadium during her historic visit in 2011. Her warm interest in the stadium and in the institution of the GAA did much to heal old wounds.

DUBLIN

is to Paris, Glasnevin is to Dublin. Here you'll find the graves of Michael Collins, Charles Stewart Parnell, and teenage rebel/martyr Kevin Barry (of patriot song fame), surrounding a replica round tower atop the crypt of Daniel O'Connell. The cemetery's 120 leafy acres are surrounded by a tall wall and a half-dozen watchtowers used to deter grave robbers. Guided tours of the cemetery are fascinating to those who love Irish culture and history. A wall of memorials commemorate all who were lost during the struggle for Irish independence a hundred years ago, including civilians and British soldiers. The adjacent museum offers more detail—you'll dig the graveyard superstitions.

Cost and Hours: Cemetery-free, museum-€6.50, €13 includes tour; daily 10:00-18:00, 1.5-hour tours hourly from 10:30 to 15:30, more in summer; tel. 01/882-6550, www.glasnevinmuseum.ie.

Getting There: It's two miles north of the city center (get here on the hop-on, hop-off bus, or take buses #40 or #140 from O'Connell Street).

Shopping in Dublin

Shops are open roughly Monday-Saturday 9:00-18:00 and until 20:00 on Thursday. Hours are shorter on Sunday (if shops are open at all). Good shopping areas include:

• **Grafton Street,** with its neighboring streets and arcades (such as the fun Great George's Arcade between Great George's and Drury Streets), and nearby shopping centers (Powerscourt Townhouse and St. Stephen's Green). Francis Street creaks with antiques.

• **Henry Street,** home to Dublin's top department stores (pedestrian-only, off O'Connell Street).

• **Nassau Street,** lining Trinity College, with the popular Kilkenny Shop (Irish design) and lots of touristy stores.

• **Temple Bar,** worth a browse for art, jewelry, New Age paraphernalia, books, music (try Claddagh Records), and gift shops. On Saturdays, a couple of markets—one for food and another for books—set up shop.

• **Millennium Walk,** a trendy lane stretching two blocks north from the River Liffey to Abbey Street. It's filled with hip restaurants, shops, and coffee bars. It's easy to miss—look for the south entry at the pedestrian Millennium Bridge, or the north entry at Jervis Street LUAS stop.

• **Street markets,** such as Moore Street (produce, noise, and lots of local color, Mon-Sat 8:00-18:00, closed Sun, near General Post Office), and St. Michan Street (food, Tue-Sat 7:00-15:00, closed Sun-Mon, behind Four Courts building).

Entertainment in Dublin

Ireland has produced some of the finest writers in the English and Irish languages, and Dublin houses some of Europe's best theaters. Though the city was the site of the first performance of Handel's *Messiah* (1742), these days Dublin is famous for the rock bands that have started here: U2, Thin Lizzy, Sinéad O'Connor, and Live Aid founder Bob Geldof's band the Boomtown Rats.

DUBLIN

Theater

Abbey Theatre is Ireland's national theater, founded by W. B. Yeats in 1904 to preserve Irish culture during British rule (performances generally nightly at 20:00, Sat matinees at 14:30, 26 Lower Abbey Street, tel. 01/878-7222, www.abbeytheatre.ie). **Gate Theatre** does foreign plays as well as Irish classics (Cavendish Row, tel. 01/874-4045, www.gatetheatre.ie). The **Gaiety Theatre** offers a wide range of quality productions (King Street South, toll tel. 0818-719-388, www.gaietytheatre.ie). The **Bord Gáis Energy Theatre** is the newest and spiffiest venue (Grand Canal Square, tel. 01/677-7999, www.bordgaisenergytheatre.ie). Intimate little **Smock Alley Theatre** hides at the western fringe of Temple Bar, offering less mainstream performances on the site of Dublin's first theater (6 Lower Exchange Street, tel. 01/677-0014, www.smockalley.com). Street theater takes the stage in Temple Bar on summer evenings. Browse the listings and fliers at the TI.

Concerts

The **3 Arena,** sited on what was once a dock railway terminus (easy LUAS access), is now sponsored by a hip phone company. Residents call it by its geographic nickname: The Point. It's considered one of the country's top live-music venues (East Link Bridge, toll tel. 01/819-8888, http://3arena.ie).

At the **National Concert Hall,** the National Symphony Orchestra performs most Friday evenings (off St. Stephen's Green at Earlsfort Terrace, tel. 01/417-0077, www.nch.ie).

Pubs and Live Traditional Music

For guided pub crawls (focusing on either Irish literature or music), see page 13.

Temple Bar and Nearby

The Temple Bar area in particular thrives with music—traditional, jazz, and pop. Although it's pricier than the rest of Dublin and extremely touristy, it really is the best place in town to mix beer and music.

Gogarty's Pub has foot-tapping sessions downstairs daily at 13:00 and upstairs nightly from 21:00 (at corner of Fleet and Anglesea, tel. 01/671-1822). Use this pub as a kickoff for your Temple Bar evening. It's also where the Traditional Irish Musical Pub Crawl starts.

The **Palace Bar** is a well-preserved gin joint, with almost 135 years of history. It attracted Dublin's literary greats from the start, and contrasts sharply (and refreshingly) with the prefab offerings down the street in the Temple Bar mayhem (east end of Temple Bar, where Fleet Street hits Westmoreland Street at 21 Fleet Street, tel. 01/671-7388, www.thepalacebardublin.com).

Porterhouse has an inviting and varied menu, Dublin's best selection of microbrews, and live music. You won't find Guinness here, just tasty homebrews. Try one of their sampler trays (corner of Essex Street East and Parliament Street, tel. 01/671-5715, check music schedule at www.theporterhouse.ie).

Near Temple Bar: A 10-minute hike up the river west of Temple Bar takes you to two pubs with a local and less touristy ambience. **The Brazen Head,** which claims to be the oldest pub in Dublin, is a hit for an early dinner and late live music (nightly from 21:30), with atmospheric rooms and a courtyard perfect for balmy evenings. They also host great "Food, Folk, and Fairies" storytelling dinner evenings. **O'Shea's Merchant Pub,** just across the street, is encrusted in memories of County Kerry football heroes. It's filled with locals taking a break from the grind. There's live traditional music nightly at 21:30 (the front half is a restaurant, the magic is in the back—enter on Bridge Street, tel. 01/679-3797, www.themerchanttemplebar.com).

More Pub Action

In Smithfield: Hiding in a nondescript building at the top of Smithfield Square north of the River Liffey, the **Cobblestone Pub** offers Dublin's least glitzy and most rewarding traditional-music venue. The candlelit walls, covered with photos of honored trad musicians, set the tone. Music is revered here, as reflected in the understated sign: "Listening area, please respect musicians" (trad-music sessions Mon-Tue at 21:00, Wed-Sat at 19:00, Sun at 14:00; 100 yards from Old Jameson Distillery's brick chimney tower at 77 King Street North, tel. 01/872-1799, www.cobblestonepub.ie).

Southeast of St. Stephen's Green: Down the axis of Merrion Row and Lower Baggot Street, you'll find three venerable pubs filled with businessmen and staff from nearby governmental buildings blowing off steam. **O'Donoghue's** was famously the home pub of the Dubliners, for decades one of Ireland's premier traditional Irish music groups. The pub still offers nightly trad sessions (15 Merrion Row, tel. 01/660-7194). **Doheny & Nesbitt** is a photogenic choice, with wonderful woodwork and cozy conversational alcoves as well as great pub grub (5 Lower Baggot Street, tel. 01/676-2945). **Toner's** is another well-varnished choice—it's already celebrated its 200th anniversary. It has the added attraction of a large beer garden out back to enjoy on fine days (139 Lower Baggot Street, tel. 01/676-3090).

Near Trinity College: The **Dingle Whiskey Bar** boasts its namesake libation but also features 170 whiskeys from Ireland, Scotland, and North America. Tasting flights are available for novice to connoisseur palates (Mon-Thu 15:00-23:00, Fri-Sun 13:00-late, 45 Naussau Street, tel. 01/644-4180).

Sleeping in Dublin

Choosing the right neighborhood in Dublin is as important as choosing the right hotel. All of my recommended accommodations are in safe areas convenient to sightseeing.

Central Dublin is popular, loud, and expensive. You'll find big, practical, central places south of the river, near Christ Church Cathedral (on the edge of Temple Bar), Trinity College, and St. Stephen's Green. For classy, older Dublin accommodations in a quieter neighborhood, stay a bit farther out, southeast of St. Stephen's Green. North of the river are a few reliable options in an urban area well-served by LUAS streetcars. If you're on a tight budget, get a room in outlying Dun Laoghaire or Howth, where rooms are cheaper—and quieter (both an easy 25-minute DART train ride into the city).

I rank accommodations from $ budget to $$$$ splurge. My recommendations include everything from €25 bunks to deluxe €270 doubles, though most of the hotels listed here cluster around €170. Prices are often discounted on weeknights (Mon-Thu) and from November through February. For some travelers, short-term, Airbnb-type rentals can be a good alternative; search for places in my recommended hotel neighborhoods.

Rooms can be tight. Book any accommodations well in advance, especially if you'll be traveling during peak season (June-August), weekends any time of year (particularly during rugby weekends), or if your trip coincides with a major holiday or festival. On Sundays in September, fans converge on Dublin from all over the country for the all-Ireland finals in Gaelic football and hurling.

To get the best deal, contact my family-run hotels directly by phone or email. By going direct, the owner avoids a roughly 20 percent commission and may be able to offer you a discount.

DUBLIN

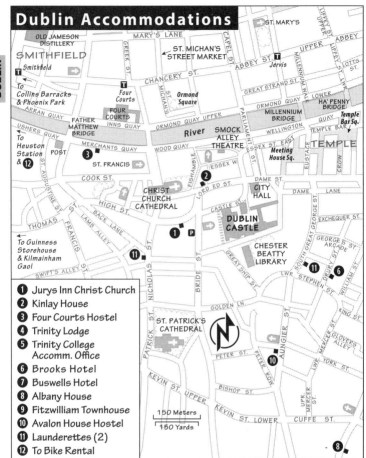

Dublin Accommodations

1. Jurys Inn Christ Church
2. Kinlay House
3. Four Courts Hostel
4. Trinity Lodge
5. Trinity College Accomm. Office
6. Brooks Hotel
7. Buswells Hotel
8. Albany House
9. Fitzwilliam Townhouse
10. Avalon House Hostel
11. Launderettes (2)
12. To Bike Rental

SOUTH OF THE RIVER LIFFEY
Near Christ Church Cathedral

These lodging options cluster near Christ Church Cathedral, a 5-minute walk from the rowdy and noisy evening scene (at Temple Bar), and 10 minutes from the sightseeing center (Trinity College and Grafton Street). The cheap hostels in this neighborhood have some double rooms. If your hotel charges extra for a full Irish breakfast, you can eat for less at the many small cafés nearby; try the Queen of Tarts or Chorus Café (see listings under "Eating in Dublin," later).

$$$$ Jurys Inn Christ Church is central and offers business-class comfort in 182 identical rooms. This no-nonsense, American-style hotel chain has a winning keep-it-simple-and-affordable

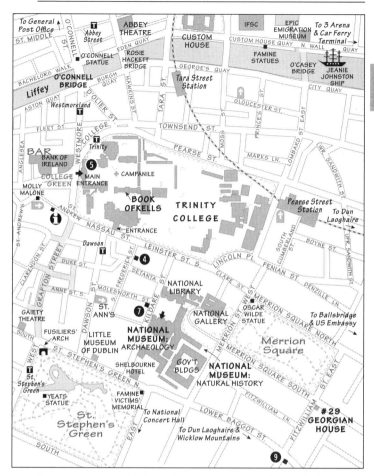

formula. If "ye olde" is getting old—and you don't mind big tour groups—this is a good option. Request a room far from the noisy elevator (breakfast extra, book long in advance for weekends, pay parking, Christ Church Place, tel. 01/454-0000, US tel. 800-423-6953, www.jurysinns.com, jurysinnchristchurch@jurysinns.com).

¢ **Kinlay House** is the backpackers' choice—definitely the place to go for cheap beds, a central location, and an all-ages-welcome atmosphere. This huge, red-brick, 19th-century Victorian building has 200 metal, prison-style beds in spartan rooms. It fills up most days—reserve well in advance, especially for summer weekends (private and family rooms available, includes continental breakfast, travel desk, kitchen, lots of stairs, Christ Church, 2 Lord Edward Street, tel. 01/679-6644, www.kinlaydublin.ie, info@kinlaydublin.ie).

¢ **Four Courts Hostel** is a 234-bed hostel well-located immediately across the river from the Four Courts. It's within a five-minute walk of Christ Church Cathedral and Temple Bar. Bare and institutional, it's also spacious and well-run, with a focus on security and efficiency (private rooms available, elevator, game room, some pay parking, 15 Merchant's Quay, from Connolly Station or Busáras Bus Station take LUAS to Four Courts stop and cross river via Father Matthew Bridge, tel. 01/672-5839, www.fourcourtshostel.com, info@fourcourtshostel.com).

Trinity College Area

You can't get more central than Trinity College; these listings offer a good value for the money.

$$$$ Trinity Lodge offers fine, quiet lodging in 26 rooms split between two Georgian townhouses on either side of South Frederick Street, just south of Trinity College (12 South Frederick Street, tel. 01/617-0900, www.trinitylodge.com, trinitylodge@eircom.net).

$$ Trinity College turns its 800 student-housing dorm rooms on campus into no-frills, affordable accommodations in the city center each summer. Look for the Accommodations Office (open Mon-Fri 8:00-18:00) through the door on the right before you come into the courtyard (rooms available late-May-mid-Sept, some en suite rooms but most with shared bath, breakfast extra, tel. 01/896-1177, www.tcd.ie/accommodation/visitors, reservations@tcd.ie).

Near St. Stephen's Green

$$$$ Brooks Hotel is a fine choice for great service, tending 98 plush rooms in an ideal central location. This splurge rarely disappoints (Drury Street, tel. 01/670-4000, www.brookshotel.ie, reservations@brookshotel.ie).

$$$$ Buswells Hotel, one of the city's oldest, is a pleasant Georgian-style haven with 67 rooms in the heart of the city (breakfast extra, between Trinity College and St. Stephen's Green at 23 Molesworth Street, tel. 01/614-6500, www.buswells.ie, info@buswells.ie).

$$$ Albany House's 50 good-value rooms come with high ceilings, Georgian ambience, and some stairs. Ask for a quieter room in back, away from streetcar noise (just one block south of St. Stephen's Green at 84 Harcourt Street, tel. 01/475-1092, www.albanyhousedublin.com, info@albanyhousedublin.com).

$$$ Fitzwilliam Townhouse rents 14 basic rooms in a Georgian townhouse near St. Stephen's Green (family rooms, breakfast extra, 41 Upper Fitzwilliam Street, tel. 01/662-5155, www.fitzwilliamtownhouse.com, info@fitzwilliamtownhouse.com).

¢ Avalon House Hostel, near Grafton Street, rents simple,

Southeast Dublin

DUBLIN
CASTLE

NASSAU ST.

TRINITY
COLLEGE

Dawson

GRAFTON ST.

St.
Stephen's
Green

NATIONAL
LIBRARY

NATIONAL
GALLERY

NATIONAL
MUSEUM:
ARCHAEOLOGY

Merrion
Square

#29
GEORGIAN
HOUSE

St.
Stephen's
Green

9

Fitzwilliam
Square

NATIONAL
CONCERT
HALL

HATCH
ST.

Harcourt

LWR. LEESON ST.

EARLSFORT TERR.

1

UPR. FITZWILLIAM ST.

WILTON
TERR.

MESPIL RD.

LWR. BAGGOT ST.

UPR.
MOUNT ST.

LWR. MOUNT ST.

Grand Canal

B

8

3

6

5

HADDINGTON RD.

PEMBROKE RD.

WATERLOO RD.

7

4

PERCY PL.

NORTHUMBERLAND RD.

RAGLAN RD.

Pearse
Street
Station

BORD GÁIS
ENERGY
THEATRE

HANOVER
QUAY

PEARSE ST.

ERNE ST.

DART
Commuter Rail

GRAND CANAL ST.

GRAND CANAL QUAY

Grand Canal
Dock Station

N

Grand Canal
Dock Station

To Aviva
Stadium
& Dun
Laoghaire

HARRINGTON ST.

200 Meters

200 Yards

Grand

GRAND
PARADE

Charlemont

GROVE RD.

CANAL RD.

UPPER
LEESON ST.

To Sandyford

To
Dun Laoghaire & Wicklow
Mountains

Accommodations
1 Number 31
2 The Schoolhouse Hotel
3 Mespil Hotel
4 Roxford Lodge Hotel
5 Waterloo House

Eateries & Pubs
6 Bloom Brasserie & Wine Bar;
   Zakura Izakaya
7 Searsons Pub & Langkawi
8 La Peniche Dinner Barge
9 O'Donoghue's; Doheny & Nesbitt;
   Toner's

clean backpacker beds (private rooms available, includes continental breakfast, elevator, a few minutes off Grafton Street at 55 Aungier Street, tel. 01/475-0001, www.avalon-house.ie, info@avalon-house.ie).

Away from the Center,
Southeast of St. Stephen's Green

The Grand Canal, Dublin's urban waterway, sports a lovely narrow greenbelt of trees and lily pads that's ideal for a pleasant stroll or jog. This neighborhood—stretching roughly east-west from Leeson Street to Grand Canal Street—is a perfect compromise between busy central lodging options and more sedate choices that are farther out. These listings are unique places (except for the business-class Mespil Hotel), and they charge accordingly. If you're going to break the bank, do it here.

$$$$ Number 31 is a hidden gem reached via gritty little Leeson Close (a lane off Lower Leeson Street). Ask Noel about the VIPs who attended dinner parties here 50 years ago. Its understated elegance is top-notch, with six rooms in a former coach house and 15 rooms in an adjacent Georgian house; the two buildings are connected by a quiet little garden. Guests appreciate the special touches (such as a sunken living room with occasional peat fires) and tasty breakfasts served in a classy glass atrium (family rooms, free parking, 31 Leeson Close, tel. 01/676-5011, www.number31. ie, info@number31.ie).

$$$$ The Schoolhouse Hotel taught as many as 300 students in its heyday (1861-1969) and was in the middle of the street fight that was the 1916 Easter Rising. Now it's a serene hideout with 31 pristine rooms and a fine restaurant (breakfast extra, book early, 2 Northumberland Road, tel. 01/667-5014, www.schoolhousehotel. com, reservations@schoolhousehotel.com).

$$$ Mespil Hotel is a huge, modern, business-class hotel renting 254 identical three-star rooms at a good price with all the comforts. This place is a cut above Jurys Inn (breakfast extra, elevator; small first-come, first-served free parking; 10-minute walk southeast of St. Stephen's Green or take bus #37, #38, #39, or #46A; 50 Mespil Road, tel. 01/488-4600, www.mespilhotel.com, mespil@leehotels.com).

$$$ Roxford Lodge Hotel is well managed and a great value. In a quiet residential neighborhood a 20-minute walk from Trinity College, it has 24 tastefully decorated rooms awash with Jacuzzis and saunas. The executive suite is honeymoon-worthy (family rooms, breakfast extra, elevator, parking, 46 Northumberland Road, tel. 01/668-8572, www.roxfordlodge.ie, reservations@ roxfordlodge.ie).

$$$ Waterloo House sits proudly Georgian on a quiet residential street with 19 comfortable and relaxing rooms and a pleasant back garden (family rooms, parking, 8 Waterloo Road, tel. 01/660-1888, www.waterloohouse.ie, info@waterloohouse.ie).

NORTH OF THE RIVER LIFFEY
Near Parnell Square

A swanky neighborhood 250 years ago, this is now workaday Dublin with a steady urban hum, made accessible by LUAS streetcars.

$$$$ The Castle Hotel is a formerly grand but still comfortable Georgian establishment embedded in the urban canyons of North Dublin. A half-block east of the Garden of Remembrance, it's a good value with pleasant rooms and the friendly Castle Vaults pub with live music in its basement (Great Denmark Street, tel. 01/874-6949, www.castle-hotel.ie, info@castle-hotel.ie).

$$$$ Jurys Inn Parnell Street has 253 predictably soulless but modern rooms. It's a block from the north end of O'Connell Street and the cluster of museums on Parnell Square (breakfast extra, tel. 01/878-4900, www.jurysinns.com, jurysinnparnellst@ jurysinns.com).

$$$$ **Belvedere Hotel** has 92 plain-vanilla rooms that are short on character but long on dependable, modern comforts (Great Denmark Street, tel. 01/873-7700, www.belvederehotel.ie, reservations@belvederehotel.ie).

$$$ **Charles Stewart Guesthouse,** big and basic, offers 60 acceptable rooms in a good location for a fair price (family rooms, breakfast extra, ask for a quieter room in the back, just beyond top end of O'Connell Street at 5 Parnell Square East, tel. 01/878-0350, www.charlesstewart.ie, info@charlesstewart.ie).

Eating in Dublin

It's easy to find fine, creative eateries all over town. While you can get decent pub grub for under €20 on just about any corner, consider saving that for the countryside. There's just no pressing reason to eat Irish in cosmopolitan Dublin. In fact, going local these days is the same as going ethnic. The city's good restaurants are packed from 19:00 on, especially on weekends. Eating early (17:30-19:00) saves time and money, as many better places offer an early-bird special. Most restaurants serve free jugs of ice water with a smile.

I rank restaurants from $ budget to $$$$ splurge.

FAST, EASY, AND CHEAP IN THE CENTER
Near Grafton Street

$$ **Cornucopia** is a small, earth-mama-with-class, proudly vegetarian, self-serve place two blocks off Grafton. It's friendly and youthful, with hearty lunches and dinner specials (daily generally until 21:00, 19 Wicklow Street, tel. 01/677-7583).

$$$ **The Farm** is a hardworking and practical place with a passion for fresh, organic, and free-range fare that's affordable and tasty. Lunch and early-bird specials are a smart value (good vegetarian options, Wed-Sat 12:00-23:00, Sun-Tue until 22:00, a half-block south of Trinity College at 3 Dawson Street, tel. 01/671-8654).

$$ **The Hairy Lemon** has a weird name, but its friendly staff, central location, and fun and creative menu keep me coming back. Hearty eaters will love their famous stew-like Dublin Coddle. Dine in the pub zone or in the brighter annex. Part of the movie *The Commitments* (1991) was filmed here (daily 11:30-22:00, 41 Lower Stephen Street, tel. 01/671-8949).

$$ **O'Neill's Pub** is a venerable, multilevel, dark, and tangled retreat offering good grub, including inexpensive breakfasts and dependable carvery lunches (daily 12:00-22:30, Suffolk Street, tel. 01/679-3656).

$$ **Avoca Café,** on the second floor above the Avoca depart-

DUBLIN

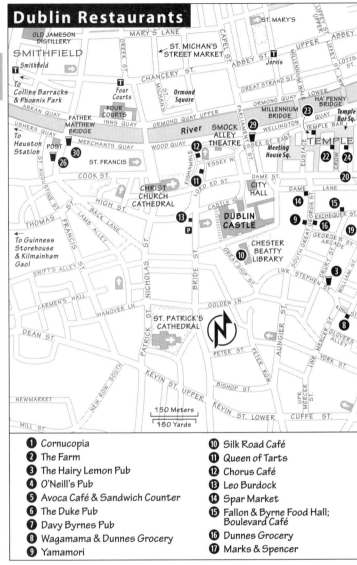

Dublin Restaurants

1	Cornucopia	**10**	Silk Road Café
2	The Farm	**11**	Queen of Tarts
3	The Hairy Lemon Pub	**12**	Chorus Café
4	O'Neill's Pub	**13**	Leo Burdock
5	Avoca Café & Sandwich Counter	**14**	Spar Market
6	The Duke Pub	**15**	Fallon & Byrne Food Hall; Boulevard Café
7	Davy Byrnes Pub	**16**	Dunnes Grocery
8	Wagamama & Dunnes Grocery	**17**	Marks & Spencer
9	Yamamori		

ment store, is a cheap and cheery eatery with healthy foodie plates, great salads, and an enthusiastic local following (Mon-Sat 9:30-17:30, Sun from 11:00, 11 Suffolk Street, tel. 01/672-6019). In the store basement, the **$ Avoca Sandwich Counter** has simple seating and a cheap buffet counter that sells food priced by weight. They also offer deli sandwiches and enticing baked goodies (great for takeaway, daily generally 10:00-18:00).

$$ The Duke and **Davy Byrnes,** neighbors on Duke Street,

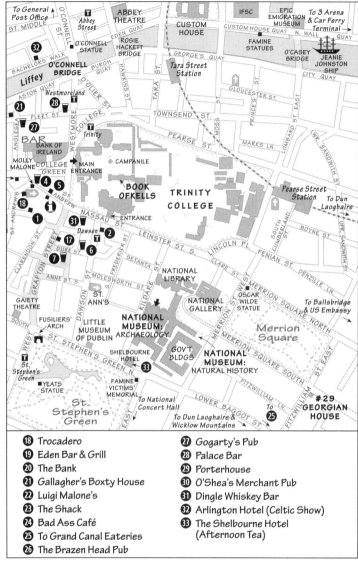

DUBLIN

18 Trocadero
19 Eden Bar & Grill
20 The Bank
21 Gallagher's Boxty House
22 Luigi Malone's
23 The Shack
24 Bad Ass Café
25 To Grand Canal Eateries
26 The Brazen Head Pub

27 Gogarty's Pub
28 Palace Bar
29 Porterhouse
30 O'Shea's Merchant Pub
31 Dingle Whiskey Bar
32 Arlington Hotel (Celtic Show)
33 The Shelbourne Hotel
(Afternoon Tea)

serve reliable pub lunches. Davy Byrnes (at #21, tel. 01/677-5217) feels like pub-meets-diner, and The Duke (at #9, tel. 01/679-9553) has a buffet counter in the back from 12:00 to 16:00. Both are favorites for Irish lit fans whose heroes frequented them (James Joyce, Brendan Behan, and Patrick Kavanagh). Davy Byrnes is where Leopold Bloom ate his gorgonzola cheese sandwich in *Ulysses*.

$$ Wagamama is a pan-Asian slurp-a-thon with great and healthy noodle and rice dishes served at long communal tables by energetic waiters (daily 12:00-22:00, South King Street underneath St. Stephen's Green Shopping Centre, tel. 01/417-1878).

$$ Yamamori is a plain, mellow, and modern Japanese place serving seas of sushi and noodles (daily 12:00-22:30, 71 South Great George's Street, tel. 01/475-5001).

Near Christ Church Cathedral

The **$ Silk Road Café** at the Chester Beatty Library serves a delightful selection of Middle Eastern and Mediterranean cuisine (in keeping with the theme of the library's collections). The dishes are always fresh, with a good variety of soups, *panini*, falafel, and vegetarian options (Mon-Fri 10:00-16:45, Sat from 11:00, Sun from 12:00, on the grounds of Dublin Castle, tel. 01/407-0770). While you're there, be sure to pop into the amazing (free) library (see listing in "Sights in Dublin").

$ Queen of Tarts, with nice outdoor seating, does yummy breakfasts, light lunches, sandwiches, and wonderful pastries (Mon-Fri 8:00-19:00, Sat-Sun from 9:00, just off Dame Street, go 100 yards up from City Hall and left on Cow's Lane, tel. 01/670-7499).

$ Chorus Café is a friendly and plain little hole-in-the-wall diner serving salads, *panini*, and pastas (daily 8:30-17:00, 7 Fishamble Street, next door to the site of the first performance of Handel's *Messiah*, tel. 01/616-7088, Cyrus).

$ Leo Burdock has been serving authentic fish-and-chips, in large splittable portions, for more than a hundred years. You'll find it around the corner from Jurys Inn—just follow the line of Dubliners waiting for their haddock (daily 12:00-23:30, no seating—takeaway only, 2 Werburgh Street, tel. 01/454-0306).

Delis and Groceries

Grocery Delis with Seating: If you want to eat fast, cheap, and healthy in the tourist center, two high-end groceries offer fresh sandwiches and a salad bar, and a place to sit while you eat. The **Spar** market (corner of Dame Street and South Great George's Street; more branches throughout the city) is open 24/7 and has huge windows overlooking the Dame Street action. The very proper **Fallon & Byrne Food Hall** is like eating at an upscale Trader Joe's (Mon-Sat 8:00-21:00, Sun until 19:00, 11 Exchequer Street).

Supermarkets: Many of Dublin's grocery stores sell cheap salads, microwaved meat pies, and made-to-order sandwiches. **Dunnes,** at 11 South Great George's Street, is your one-stop shop for assembling a picnic meal (Mon-Sat 8:30-19:00, Sun from 11:00). They have another outlet in the basement of St. Stephen's Green Shopping Centre. **Marks & Spencer** department store has a fancy grocery store in the basement, with fine takeaway sandwiches and salads (daily 8:00-20:00, 20 Grafton Street). **Centra** markets, some open 24 hours, are spread all over Dublin.

HIP AND FUN IN NORTH DUBLIN

The Church is a trendy café/bar/restaurant/nightclub/beer garden housed in the former St. Mary's Church. In its former life as a church, it hosted the baptism of Irish rebel Wolfe Tone and the marriage of brewing legend Arthur Guinness. The **$$$ choir balcony** has a huge pipe organ and a refined menu (daily 17:00-22:30). The ground floor **$$ nave** is dominated by a long bar and pub grub (daily 12:00-21:00). A disco thumps away in the bunker-like basement. On warm summer nights, the outdoor terrace is packed. Eating here is as much about the scene as the cuisine (reservations smart Fri and Sat nights, corner of St. Mary's and Jervis Streets, tel. 01/828-0102, www.thechurch.ie).

$$$ Mr Fox is an elegant and serene little basement operation serving locally sourced dishes created by chef Anthony Smith (Tue-Fri 12:00-14:00 & 17:00-21:30, Sat 17:30-22:00, closed Sun-Mon; behind the Garden of Remembrance at 38 Parnell Square West, tel. 01/874-7778, www.mrfox.ie).

$$ Brannigan's is an inviting and family-run traditional pub—it's been a "beer emporium since 1909." They offer a non-touristy lunch buffet (Mon-Fri 12:00-15:00), and it's convenient for theatergoers—located roughly halfway between the Gate and Abbey theaters (daily 10:30-23:30, 9 Cathedral Street, just off O'Connell Street 50 yards from the Spire, tel. 01/874-0137).

CLASSY DINING SOUTH OF TEMPLE BAR

These stylish restaurants serve well-presented food at fair prices. They're located within a block of each other, just south of Temple Bar and Dame Street, near the main TI.

$$$$ Trocadero serves beefy European cuisine to Dubliners interested in a slow, romantic meal. The dressy, red-velvet interior is draped with photos of local actors. Come early or make a reservation—it's a favorite with theatergoers (Mon-Sat 17:00-23:30, closed Sun, 4 St. Andrew Street, tel. 01/677-5545, www.trocadero.ie). The three-course pretheater special is a fine value at €27 (17:00-19:00, leave by 19:45, Robert).

$$$ Eden Bar & Grill lurks on funky William Street with a varied menu from monkfish to pizza, highlighted by especially creative lamb dishes (daily 12:00-16:00 & 17:30-22:00, 7 South William Street, tel. 01/670-6887).

$$$ Boulevard Café is mod, trendy, and likeable, dishing up Mediterranean cuisine that's heavy on the Italian. It's smart to reserve for dinner (Mon-Sat 12:00-22:00, Sun 12:30-20:00, 27 Exchequer Street, tel. 01/679-2131, www.boulevardcafe.ie).

$$$ **The Bank** wows visitors with its grand Victorian bank-lobby ambience, lit by an arched Tiffany skylight. You'll find great food—the mussel and oyster starters are a hit—in a central location (daily 11:00-23:30, 20 College Green, tel. 01/677-0677).

IN TEMPLE BAR

$$ **Gallagher's Boxty House** is touristy and traditional—a good, basic value with creaky floorboards and old Dublin ambience. They serve stews and corned beef, but the specialty is boxty, the generally bland-tasting Irish potato pancake filled and rolled with various meats, veggies, and sauces (Mon-Fri 12:00-22:00, Sat-Sun from 11:00, reservations wise, 20 Temple Bar, tel. 01/677-2762, www.boxtyhouse.ie).

$$ **Luigi Malone's,** with its fun atmosphere and varied menu of pizza, ribs, pasta, sandwiches, and fajitas, is just the place to take your high-school date (Mon-Sat 12:00-22:00, Sun 13:00-21:30, corner of Cecilia and Fownes streets, tel. 01/679-2723).

$$$ **The Shack,** while touristy, has a reputation for good quality. It serves traditional Irish, chicken, seafood, and steak dishes (daily 12:00-22:00, in the center of Temple Bar, 24 East Essex Street, tel. 01/679-0043).

The $$ **Bad Ass Café** serves pizza, pasta, burgers, and salads that are cheap by Temple Bar standards. There's even a fun kids' menu. Their big patio fronts the Temple Bar action, and there's live music nightly in the dark, sprawling, pubby interior (daily 12:00-22:00, 9 Crown Alley, tel. 01/675-3005).

NEAR THE GRAND CANAL

These places are within a long block of one other in the emerging Grand Canal neighborhood—an area southeast of St. Stephen's Green that's (as yet) undiscovered by the tourist crowds. You'll find them just over the Grand Canal about a 20-minute walk from the center (near the intersection of Baggot Street and Mespil Road).

$$$ **Bloom Brasserie & Wine Bar** has a woody, candlelit ambience with beautifully presented dishes based on locally sourced meats (beef, lamb, duck) and seafood (Irish salmon). The modern menu changes with the seasons (Mon-Sat 12:00-14:30 & 17:00-22:30, closed Sun, 11 Upper Baggot Street, tel. 01/668-7170).

$$ **Searsons Pub,** a sprawling neighborhood favorite, is a gastropub with an open kitchen, a classy-for-a-sports-bar energy, and friendly service. If there's a horse race or rugby match on, it'll be on the screens here (it's located near the rugby stadium and a bet-

ting office). You can escape the clamor out back on the patio (daily 12:00-23:30, 42 Upper Baggot Street, tel. 01/660-0330).

$$ Zakura Izakaya is a classy-if-noisy Japanese place—small and tight, like a sushi wine-bar (daily 12:00-22:00, 7 Upper Baggot Street, tel. 01/563-8000).

$$ Langkawi is a cozy, traditional family operation serving Malaysian fusion food, with spicy Indian influences and rice-based Chinese favorites (daily 12:30-14:00 & 18:00-23:30, 46 Upper Baggot Street, tel. 01/668-2760).

$$$$ La Peniche is a floating barge sailing relaxed diners slowly up the leafy Grand Canal on twice-evening departures. Their French-inspired dishes, served in a novel nautical setting, are unique among Dublin dining experiences. While the seating is tight, it's a romantic meal. The boat moves very slowly—just a couple of hundred yards—and if it's dark, there's no real view (daily at 18:00 and 21:00, reservations smart, Grand Canal Jetty, mobile 087-790-0077, www.lapeniche.ie).

DINNER WITH ENTERTAINMENT

$$$$ The Brazen Head hosts "Food, Folk and Fairies" evenings, which are more culturally highbrow than the title might suggest, while still remaining fun. Even at €48, the evening is a great value. You get a hearty, four-course meal that's punctuated between courses by soulful Irish history and fascinating Irish mythology, delivered by an engaging local folklorist, with occasional live trad tunes in-between (daily 19:00-22:00, Jan-Feb Thu and Sat only; reservations smart; by south end of Father Matthew Bridge, 2 blocks west of Christ Church Cathedral at 20 Bridge Street; pub tel. 01/677-9549, show tel. 01/218-8555, www.irishfolktours.com).

The **$$$$ Musical Pub Crawl Dinner Show** is a handy intro to Irish traditional music and dancing. Two accomplished musicians take time between tunes to humorously point out what makes this music uniquely Irish—it's a great primer. Then you'll move on to dinner with Irish dancing as part of the entertainment (€43, May-Sept Tue-Sat at 18:00, meet at Oliver St. John's Gogarty's on Fleet Street in Temple Bar, tel. 01/475-8345, www.musicalpubcrawl.com).

$$$ Celtic Nights combines traditional music and dancing into a big-stage, high-energy, family-friendly, Irish variety show. This touristy dinner act hits all the clichés, from *Riverdance*-style choreography to fun fiddling and comedic *craic*. It comes with a traditional three-course dinner and lots of audience participation (€35, €15 for children under 12, nightly show at 20:30, downtown by the O'Connell Bridge at the Arlington Hotel, 23 Bachelors Walk, tel. 01/687-5200, www.celticnights.com).

AFTERNOON TEA

$$$$ The Shelbourne Hotel has been a Dublin landmark since 1824, built to attract genteel patrons and Dublin's upper-crust socialites (not to mention British Army snipers during the 1916 Easter Rising). But schlubs like us can dip our toes in the aristocratic fantasy by enjoying the tradition of afternoon tea (no shorts, tank tops, or T-shirts). The menu is a swirl of finger sandwiches, buttermilk scones, clotted cream, strawberry jam, ginger loaf, and fine coffee...as well as 22 varieties of tea. You'll find it in the ground floor Lord Mayor's Lounge (seatings Mon-Thu at 13:00, 15:15, and 17:30; Fri-Sun at 11:45, 14:00, 16:15, and 18:30; reservations smart, especially on weekends; 27 St. Stephen's Green, tel. 01/663-4500).

Dublin Connections

BY PLANE

Dublin Airport has two terminals located an easily walkable 150 yards apart (airport code: DUB, tel. 01/814-1111, www.dublinairport.ie). Both have ATMs, cafés, Wi-Fi, and luggage storage (www.leftluggage.ie). There is no TI at the airport.

Getting Downtown by Bus: You have two main choices—Airlink (double-decker turquoise bus) or Aircoach (single-deck blue bus). Both pick up on the street directly in front of arrivals, at ground level at both terminals.

Airlink Express: Airlink bus #747 generally runs an east-west route that parallels the River Liffey, and includes stops at the Busáras Central Bus Station, Connolly Station, O'Connell Street, Temple Bar, Christ Church, and Heuston Station. Airlink bus #757 links the airport to the center along a generally north-south axis, including Trinity College, St. Stephen's Green (eastern end), and the National Concert Hall. Ask the driver which stop is closest to your hotel (€7, pay driver, 3-5/hour, about 40 minutes; runs Mon-Sat 5:45-late, Sun from 7:00; tel. 01/873-4222, www.dublinbus.ie). This bus is covered by the Leap Visitor and the Do Dublin transit cards; both cards can be purchased at the airport.

Aircoach: This bus generally runs a north-south route that follows the O'Connell and Grafton streets axis. To reach recommended hotels south of the city center, the Aircoach bus #700 or #703 work well (€7 if paying driver, €6 if booked online, covered by Dublin Pass, 3/hour, fewer late-night, runs 24 hours, tel. 01/844-7118, www.aircoach.ie).

By Taxi: Taxis from the airport into Dublin cost about €30.

Sleeping at the Airport: A safe bet is the **$$$ Radisson Blu Dublin Airport** (tel. 01/844-6000, www.radissonblu.ie).

BY TRAIN OR BUS

The frequencies listed below are for Monday-Saturday. Trains and buses generally run less frequently on Sundays.

By Train from Dublin's Heuston Station to: Tralee (every two hours, most change in Mallow but one direct evening train, 4 hours), **Ennis** (11/day, 3-4 hours, change in Limerick, Limerick Junction, or Athenry), **Galway** (8/day, 3 hours), **Westport** (5/day, 3 hours). Irish Rail train info: Toll tel. 1850-366-222, www.irishrail.ie.

By Train from Dublin's Connolly Station to: Rosslare (3-4/day, 3 hours), **Portrush** (7/day, 5 hours, transfer in Belfast or Coleraine). The **Dublin-Belfast train** connects the capitals in two hours at 90 mph (8/day Mon-Sat, 5/day Sun). Northern Ireland train info: Tel. 048/9089-9400, www.translink.co.uk.

By Bus to: Belfast (hourly, most via Dublin Airport, 3 hours), **Trim** (almost hourly, 1 hour), **Ennis** (almost hourly, 5 hours), **Galway** (hourly, 3.5 hours; faster on CityLink—hourly, 2.5 hours, tel. 091/564-164, www.citylink.ie), **Westport** (6/day, 5 hours), **Limerick** (7/day, 3.5 hours), **Tralee** (7/day, 6 hours), **Dingle** (4/day, 8.5 hours, transfer at Limerick and Tralee). Bus info: Toll tel. 1850-836-611, www.buseireann.ie.

BY CAR

It's best to avoid driving in hectic Dublin. If you plan to drive in Ireland, save your car rental for the countryside. Consider renting a car at the airport, where you'll find all the standard car-rental agencies with longer hours and easier access to the M-50.

M-50 Toll Road: Drivers renting a car at Dublin Airport and heading for the countryside can bypass the worst of the big-city traffic by taking the M-50 ring road south or west. The M-50 uses an automatic tolling system called eFlow. Your rental should come with an eFlow tag installed; confirm this when you pick up your car. The €3.10 toll per trip is automatically debited from the credit card with which you rented the car (for pass details, see www.eflow.ie).

Other Toll Roads: Your rental car's eFlow tag will work only for the M-50 ring road around Dublin. On any other Irish toll roads, you'll have to pay with cash (about €2/toll). These roads mostly run outward from Dublin toward Waterford, Cork, Limerick, and Galway (roads farther west are free).

CONNECTING IRELAND AND BRITAIN

It's worth spending a few minutes researching your transportation options across the Irish Sea. Most airline and ferry companies routinely offer online discounts. Before sorting out rail/ferry prices with individual companies, try www.arrivatrainswales.co.uk/sailrail, which deals with several companies and has fares

DUBLIN

low enough to compete with cheap airlines. Ferries work for rural Wales or Scotland; for everywhere else, fly.

Flights: If you're going directly to London, flying is your best bet. Ryanair and Aer Lingus are the predominant discount carriers, but note that their London-bound flights often land at Luton or Stansted—airports some distance from the city center. If you need to get to Heathrow, try British Airways; some Aer Lingus flights land there, too.

Ferries: Irish Ferries and Stena Line combine to make eight daily crossings between Dublin Port (two miles east of O'Connell Bridge) and Holyhead, Wales. Most trips take 3.5 hours (€39), but Irish Ferries offers a twice-daily fast boat that makes the trip in 2 hours (€44). You must board at least 30 minutes before the scheduled sailing time. Since these boats can fill up on summer weekends, book at least a week ahead during the peak period.

Irish Ferries depart at 2:40, 11:50, 14:10, and 17:15 (Dublin tel. 0818-300-400, UK tel. 08717-300-400, www.irishferries.com); Stena Line sails at 2:15, 8:20, 15:10, and 20:40 (Dublin tel. 01/907-5555, UK tel. 08447-707-070, www.stenaline.ie).

Dublin Bay

Dangling from opposite ends of Dublin Bay's crescent-shaped shoreline, Dun Laoghaire (dun LEERY) and Howth (rhymes with "growth") are two peas in a pod. They offer quiet, cheaper lodging alternatives to Dublin and have easy light-rail access to the city center, just a 25-minute ride away. Dun Laoghaire is bigger and has more going on, while Howth has a sleepier vibe and a fishing fleet.

Dun Laoghaire

Dun Laoghaire is seven miles south of Dublin. This snoozy suburb, with easy connections to downtown Dublin, is a convenient small-town base for exploring the big city.

The Dun Laoghaire harbor was strategic enough to merit a line of martello towers, built in 1804 to defend against an expected Napoleonic invasion (one tower now houses the James Joyce Museum). By the mid-19th century, massive breakwaters were completed to pro-

tect the huge harbor. Ships
sailed regularly from here to
Wales (75 miles away), and
the first train line in Ireland connected the termi-
nal with Dublin. Since the
ferries left, Dun Laoghaire
has gotten quieter, and it no
longer has a TI.

GETTING TO DUN LAOGHAIRE

The DART commuter train connects to Dublin in 25 minutes (4/
hour, runs daily until about 23:30, €3.25 one-way, €6.15 round-
trips are good same day only, www.irishrail.ie). If you're coming
from Dublin, catch a DART train marked *Bray* or *Greystones* and
get off at the Sandycove/Glasthule or Dun Laoghaire stop, depending on your B&B's location. If you're leaving Dun Laoghaire,
catch a train marked *Howth* to get to Dublin. Get off at the central
Tara Street Station to sightsee in Dublin, or, for train connections
north, ride one stop farther to Connolly Station.

Aircoach bus #703 makes it easy to connect Dun Laoghaire
and Dublin Airport. To return to the airport from Dun Laoghaire,
catch the bus by the Pavilion Theatre on Marine Road or at the
front steps of the Royal Marine Hotel (€10, runs hourly, 50 minutes, tel. 01/844-7118, www.aircoach.ie).

With the DART and Aircoach options, taking a taxi is like
throwing money away. But if you really need one, try ABC Taxi
service (about €30 to Dublin, €40 to the airport, tel. 01/285-5444).

Dun Laoghaire is ideal for those who want to leave their cars
and sightsee Dublin by DART, as parking is cheap and sometimes free (pay-and-display parking enforced Mon-Sat 8:00-19:00,
€1.50/hour, 3-hour maximum, free on Sun).

Orientation to Dun Laoghaire

Once a busy transportation hub, Dun Laoghaire has a coastline
defined by its nearly mile-long breakwaters—reaching like two
muscular arms into the Irish Sea. The breakwaters are popular for
strollers, bikers, bird-watchers, and fishermen.

Helpful Hints: For **laundry,** try Q-Clean, located in the village of Glasthule, a five-minute downhill walk from Sandycove/
Glasthule DART station (full-service only, Mon-Sat 9:00-18:00,
closed Sun, 34 Glasthule Road, tel. 01/230-1120). For the **best
views,** hike out to the lighthouse (at the end of the East Pier) or
climb the tight stairs to the top of the James Joyce Tower and Museum.

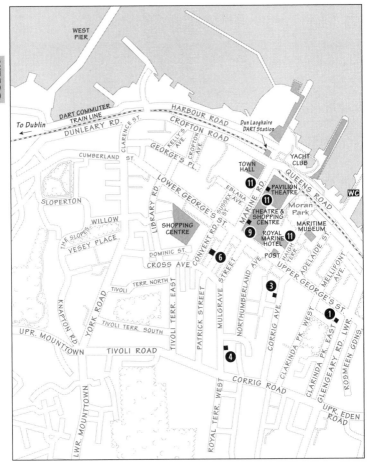

Sights in Dun Laoghaire

James Joyce Tower and Museum

This squat martello tower at Sandycove was originally built to repel a possible Napoleonic invasion, but it became famous chiefly because of its association with James Joyce. The great author lived here briefly and made it the setting for the opening of his novel *Ulysses*. The museum's round exhibition space is filled with literary memorabilia, including photographs and rare first editions. For a fine view, climb the claustrophobic, two-story spiral stairwell sealed inside the thick wall to reach the rooftop gun mount.

Cost and Hours: Free, daily 10:00-18:00, Nov-Feb until 16:00; the museum is run by volunteers—call ahead to be sure it's open, tel. 01/280-9265, www.joycetower.ie.

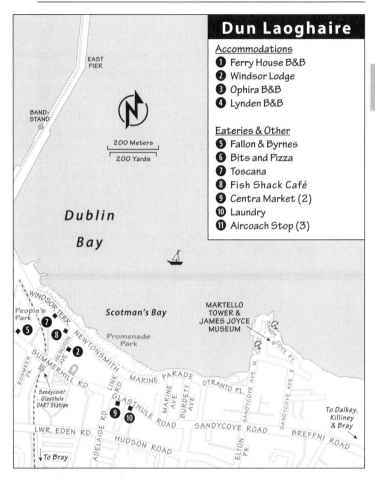

National Maritime Museum of Ireland

Maritime exhibits fill a former church with model steamships, brass fittings, accounts of heroic rescue attempts, and a huge lighthouse optic (lamp lens, installed where the altar once stood). Landlubbers may find it underwhelming.

Cost and Hours: €6, daily 11:00-17:00, Haigh Terrace, tel. 01/214-3964, www.mariner.ie.

Plays and Concerts

The Pavilion Theatre offers performances in the center of town (box office open Mon-Sat 12:00-17:00, open 2 hours before performances, Marine Road, tel. 01/231-2929, www.paviliontheatre.ie).

Swimming

Kids of all ages enjoy swimming at the safe, sandy little cove bordered by rounded rocks beside the martello tower.

Sleeping in Dun Laoghaire

The first two places are near the Sandycove/Glasthule DART Station; the last two places are near the Dun Laoghaire DART Station.

$$ Ferry House B&B, with four high-ceilinged rooms, is a family-friendly place on a dead-end street (family room, 15 Clarinda Park North just off Clarinda Park West, tel. 01/280-8301, mobile 087-267-0511, www.ferryhousedublin.ie, ferry_house@hotmail.com, Eamon and Pauline Teehan).

$ Windsor Lodge rents four fresh, inviting rooms on a quiet street a block off the harbor and a block from the DART station (cash only, 3 Islington Avenue, tel. 01/284-6952, mobile 086-844-6646, www.windsorlodge.ie, windsorlodgedublin@gmail.com, Mary O'Farrell).

$ Ophira B&B is a historic house with four comfortably creaky rooms run by active diver-hiker-biker John O'Connor and his wife, Cathy (family room, parking, 10 Corrig Avenue, tel. 01/280-0997, www.ophira.ie, johnandcathy@ophira.ie).

$ Lynden B&B, with a classy 180-year-old interior hiding behind a somber front, rents four big rooms (cash only, cheaper rooms with shared bath, go past Mulgrave Street to 2 Mulgrave Terrace, tel. 01/280-6404, www.lyndenbandb.com, mariatgavin@gmail.com, Maria Gavin).

Eating in Dun Laoghaire

George's Street—Dun Laoghaire's main drag, three blocks inland—has plenty of reasonably priced eateries and pubs, many with live music.

$$ Fallon & Byrnes is your best bet for fine wine and good food in a lovely glassed-in space beside the pleasant People's Park (daily 12:00-21:00, Summerhill Road, tel. 01/230-3300).

$$ Bits and Pizza is kid-friendly and a good bet for families (daily 12:00-22:00, off George's Street at 15 Patrick Street, tel. 01/284-2411).

$$ Toscana, on the seafront, is a popular little cubbyhole, serving hearty Italian dishes and pizza. Its location makes it easy to incorporate into your evening stroll. Reserve for dinner (early-bird specials before 18:30, daily 12:00-22:00, 5 Windsor Terrace, tel. 01/230-0890, http://toscana.ie).

$$ Fish Shack Café, on the stroll-worthy waterfront, serves fresh fish dishes to beachcombers (daily 12:00-22:00, takeout available, 1 Martello Terrace, tel. 01/284-4555).

Groceries: For picnic shopping, try **Centra Market,** right on Marine Road (daily until 22:00).

In Glasthule: Called simply "the village" locally, Glasthule is just down the street from the Sandycove/Glasthule DART station and has an array of fun, hardworking little restaurants plus a Centra Market.

Howth

Eight miles north of Dublin, Howth rests on a teardrop-shaped peninsula that pokes the Irish Sea. Its active harbor chugs with fishing boats earnestly bringing in the daily catch, and seals trolling for scraps. Weary Dubliners come here for refreshing coastal cliff walks near the city. Located at the north  terminus of the DART light-rail line, Howth makes a good place for travelers to settle in, with easy connections to Dublin for sightseeing. But there are only a couple centrally located and worthwhile lodging options.

Howth was once an important gateway to Dublin. Near the neck of the peninsula is the suburb of Clontarf, where Irish High King Brian Boru defeated the last concerted Viking attack in 1014. Eight hundred years later, a squat martello tower was built on a bluff above Howth's harbor to defend it from a Napoleonic invasion that never came. The harbor then grew as a port for shipping from Liverpool and Wales. It was eventually eclipsed by Dun Laoghaire, which was first to gain rail access. Irish rebels smuggled German-supplied guns into Ireland via Howth in 1914, making the 1916 Easter Rising possible. Soon after, Howth became a favorite safe-house refuge for rebel mastermind Michael Collins. These days, this is a pleasant, coastal hamlet.

GETTING TO HOWTH

The DART light-rail system zaps travelers between Howth and the city (4/hour, 25 minutes, daily until about 23:30, €3.25 one-way, €6.15 round-trips good same day only, www.irishrail.ie). If you're coming from Dublin, catch a DART train marked *Howth* (not *Howth Junction, Malahide,* or *Drogheda*) and ride it to the end of the line—passing through Howth Junction en route. All trains departing Howth head straight to Dublin's Connolly Station, and then continue on to Tara and Pearse stations (get off at Tara for most sightseeing). Grab a morning train to minimize the jam on sunny summer weekends.

A taxi from the airport takes about 20 minutes and costs about €25. Try Executive Cabs (tel. 01/839-6020).

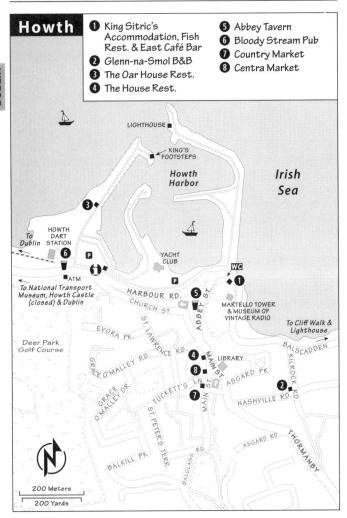

Howth

1. King Sitric's Accommodation, Fish Rest. & East Café Bar
2. Glenn-na-Smol B&B
3. The Oar House Rest.
4. The House Rest.
5. Abbey Tavern
6. Bloody Stream Pub
7. Country Market
8. Centra Market

LIGHTHOUSE

KING'S FOOTSTEPS

Howth Harbor

Irish Sea

To Dublin

HOWTH DART STATION

To National Transport Museum, Howth Castle (closed) & Dublin

ATM

YACHT CLUB

HARBOUR RD.

CHURCH ST.

WC

MARTELLO TOWER & MUSEUM OF VINTAGE RADIO

To Cliff Walk & Lighthouse

EVORA PK.

ST. LAWRENCE RD.

ABBEY ST.

BALSCADDEN

Deer Park Golf Course

GRACE O'MALLEY RD.

LIBRARY

MAIN ST.

ASGARD PK.

KILROCK RD.

GRACE O'MALLEY DR.

TUCKETT'S LN.

NASHVILLE RD.

THORMANBY

ST. PETER'S TERR.

BALGLASS RD.

ASGARD RD.

BALKILL PK.

N

200 Meters
200 Yards

Orientation to Howth

Howth perches on the north shore of the peninsula and generally divides along the east-west harborfront and the north-south street that winds uphill to the village.

The quarter-mile harborfront promenade stretches from the DART station (in the west) to the martello tower on the bluff (in the east). Dominating the view are two stony piers that clutch like crab claws at the Irish Sea. The West Pier has the fishing action, while the East Pier extends to a stubby 200-year-old lighthouse and views of a rugged nearby island, Ireland's Eye. The village is reached via Abbey Street (becoming Main Street), extending uphill from the harbor near the base of the martello tower bluff. Along the street, you'll find a church, most of the shops and pubs, and a grocery store.

There are two **ATMs** in town: the tiny Ulster Bank kiosk across the street from the DART station (to the left of the Gem Market) and inside the Centra Market. The helpful **TI** is located on the harborfront, in a tiny wooden hut on Harbour Road, across from Howth's old courthouse (daily 9:30-17:00, shorter hours off-season, tel. 085/858-1695, www.howthismagic.com).

Sights in Howth

Other than coastal walks, sightseeing here pales in comparison to Dublin. Privately owned Howth Castle cannot be toured.

Museum of Vintage Radio

The three-story martello tower on the bluff overlooking the East Pier is the only sight in Howth worth a glance. Curator Pat Herbert has spent decades acquiring his collection of lovingly preserved radios, phonographs, and even a hurdy-gurdy (a crank-action musical oddity)—all of which still work. Check out the radio disguised as a picture frame, which was used by the resistance in occupied France during World War II.

Before leaving the compact bluff, catch the views of the harbor and the nearby island of Ireland's Eye. Spot the distant martello tower on the island's west end and the white guano coating its eastern side, courtesy of a colony of gannets.

Cost and Hours: €5, daily 11:00-16:00, Sat-Sun only Nov-April, entry up driveway off Abbey Street, mobile 086-815-4189.

National Transport Museum

Housed in a large shed on the castle grounds, this is a dusty waste of time unless you find rapture in old trams and buses (€3, Sat-Sun only 14:00-17:00, tel. 01/848-0831, www.nationaltransportmuseum. org).

St. Mary's Abbey

Looming above Abbey Street, the abbey ruins date from the early 1400s. Before that, a church built by Norse King Sitric in 1042 stood at this site. The entrance to the ruins is on Church Street, above the abbey grounds.

East and West Piers

The piers make for mellow strolls after a meal. Poke your head into the various fishmonger shops along the West Pier to see the day's catch. At the end of the pier (on the leeward side), you'll find the footprints of King George IV carved into the stone after his

1821 visit. The East Pier is a quiet jetty barbed with a squat lighthouse and the closest views of Ireland's Eye. If you want to get even closer to the island, book a boat excursion (€15 round-trip, daily in summer on demand 10:30-18:00, call for off-season trips, mobile 086-845-9154, www. islandferries.net).

Hiking Trails

Trails above the eastern cliffs of the peninsula offer enjoyable, breezy exercise. For a scenic three-hour round-trip, walk past the East Pier and martello tower, following Balscadden Road uphill. You'll soon pass Balscadden House, where writer W. B. Yeats spent part of his youth (watch for plaque on left). A 10-minute stroll beyond that, the road dead-ends, where you'll find the well-marked trailhead and easy-to-follow trail; soon you'll be walking south around the craggy coastline to grand views of the Bailey Lighthouse on the southeast rim of the peninsula. The gate to the lighthouse grounds is always locked, so enjoy the view from afar before retracing your steps back to Howth.

Sleeping in Howth

$$$$ King Sitric's Accommodation is Howth's best lodging option and has a fine harborfront seafood restaurant. It fills the old harbormaster's house with eight well-kept rooms and a friendly staff (discounts for 2-night stay with dinner, East Pier below martello tower, tel. 01/832-5235, www.kingsitric.ie, info@kingsitric. ie, Aidan and Joan MacManus).

$ Glenn-na-Smol B&B is a homey house with six unpretentious rooms in a quiet setting, a 15-minute walk uphill along the coast behind the martello tower (family room, cash only, parking, corner of Nashville Road & Kilrock Road, tel. 01/832-2936, mobile 085-758-1083, rickards@indigo.ie, Sean and Margaret Rickard).

Eating in Howth

$$$$ King Sitric's Fish Restaurant, one of the area's most famous seafood experiences, serves Irish versions of French classics in a dining room (upstairs) with harbor views. Chef Aidan Mac-Manus rises early each morning to select the best of the day's catch on the pier to be enjoyed that evening (Wed-Sat 18:00-21:30,

Sun 13:00-17:00, closed Mon-Tue, reservations a good idea, tel. 01/832-5235, www.kingsitric.ie). They also operate the more economical **$$ East Café Bar** on the ground floor with extra seating out front. Their soups, salads, steak sandwiches, and fish dishes are a good value (daily 10:00-22:00).

$$$ The Oar House sits halfway down the West Pier, serving a variety of fresh fish dishes in a bustling atmosphere (daily 12:00-"the cows come home," 8 West Pier, tel. 01/839-4568).

$$$ The House is the best value up the hill in the village. Here you'll find a comfortable local vibe, a contemporary creative menu, and a rumor that Captain Bligh once lodged here (Tue-Sun 12:00-21:00, Mon open for lunch only, 4 Main Street, tel. 01/839-6388).

For standard pub grub, try the **$$ Abbey Tavern** up the hill on Abbey Street (occasional trad music and dance, call for schedule, tel. 01/839-0307). Another good choice is the **$$ Bloody Stream Pub** in front of the DART station (tel. 01/839-5076). The **Country Market** sells picnic supplies, and its cheap and friendly upstairs tearoom offers lunch (daily 9:00-18:00, Main Street). The **Centra Market** is a block closer to the waterfront (daily until 22:00, Main Street).

NEAR DUBLIN

Boyne Valley • Trim • Glendalough • Wicklow Mountains • Irish National Stud

Not far from urban Dublin, the stony skeletons of evocative ruins sprout from the lush Irish countryside. The story of Irish history is told by ancient burial mounds, early Christian monastic settlements, huge Norman castles, and pampered estate gardens. In gentler inland terrain, the Irish love of equestrian sport is nurtured in grassy pastures ruled by spirited thoroughbreds. These sights are separated into three regions: north of Dublin (the Boyne Valley, including Brú na Bóinne and the town of Trim), south of Dublin (Powerscourt Estate Gardens, Glendalough, and the Wicklow Mountains), and west of Dublin (the Irish National Stud).

Boyne Valley

The peaceful, green Boyne Valley, just 30 miles north of Dublin, has an impressive concentration of historical and spiritual sights: The enigmatic burial mounds at Brú na Bóinne are older than the Egyptian pyramids. At the Hill of Tara (seat of the high kings of Celtic Ireland), St. Patrick preached his most persuasive sermon. The valley also contains the first monastery in Ireland and several of the country's finest high crosses. You'll see Trim's 13th-century castle—Ireland's biggest—built by Norman invaders, and you can wander the site of the historic Battle of the Boyne (1690), which cemented Protestant British domination over Catholic Ireland until the 20th century.

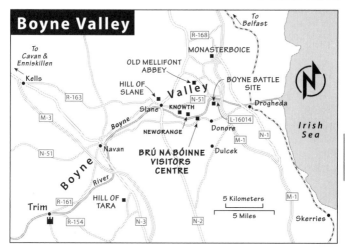

PLANNING YOUR TIME

Of these sights, only Brú na Bóinne is worth ▲▲▲ (and deserves a good three hours). The others, while relatively meager physically, are powerfully evocative to anyone interested in Irish history and culture. If you have a car, get an early start, and eat your Weetabix, you could see the entire region in a day.

As you plan your Ireland itinerary, if you're flying into or out of Dublin but want to avoid the intensity and expense of that big city, consider using Trim as an overnight base (45-minute drive from airport) and tour these sights from there.

GETTING AROUND BOYNE VALLEY

The region is a joy by car, because all of the described sights are within a 30-minute drive of one another. Though the sights are on tiny roads, they're well-marked with brown, tourist-friendly road signs. You'll navigate best using an Ordnance Survey atlas.

It's also possible to get to the Boyne Valley from Dublin with a tour. **Newgrange Tours** visits Brú na Bóinne (including inside the Newgrange tomb), the Hill of Tara, and the Hill of Slane in a seven-hour trip (€40, daily pickup from several Dublin hotels, book direct via website, mobile 086-355-1355, www.newgrangetours.com, newgrangetours@gmail.com).

Brú na Bóinne

The famous archaeological site of Brú na Bóinne—"dwelling place of the Boyne"—is also commonly called "Newgrange," after its star attraction. Here you can visit two ▲▲▲ 5,000-year-old passage tombs—**Newgrange** and **Knowth** (rhymes with "south"). These are massive grass-covered burial mounds built atop separate hills, with a chamber inside reached by a narrow stone passage. Mysterious, thought-provoking, and mind-bogglingly old, these tombs can give you chills.

GETTING THERE

By **car,** drive 45 minutes north from Dublin on N-1 to Drogheda, where signs direct you to the visitors center. If you're using a GPS, input "Brú na Bóinne" rather than "Newgrange" to get to the visitors center, where you must check in.

Without a car, you can combine **train and taxi** service. First take a train departing Dublin Connolly station at 8:00, which puts you in the town of Drogheda around 9:00 (€12 round-trip; confirm train times at www.irishrail.ie). From here it's a short taxi ride to the Brú na Bóinne visitors center (approximately €8 one-way).

PLANNING YOUR VISIT

Access to Newgrange and Knowth is by guided tour only. You'll start your visit at the state-of-the-art visitors center with its excellent museum, then catch a shuttle bus to the tomb sites, where a guide gives a 30-minute tour.

Each tomb site takes about 1.5 hours to visit (30-minute round-trip bus ride plus 30-minute guided tour plus 30 minutes of free time). The museum at the visitors center is well worth an additional 30-60 minutes. If you add in waiting time for the next available shuttle bus, you're looking at a minimum of 2.5 hours to visit one of the tombs (along with the museum), or 4 hours to visit both tombs (and museum).

Which tomb is best? If you can't see both, I'd pick Newgrange because it's more famous and allows you inside. (On the other hand, wait times for the Newgrange shuttle bus can be longer.) Knowth is bigger and flanked by small mounds, but you can't access its narrow passages. Each site is different enough and worthwhile, but for many, seeing just one is adequate. You might pick your tomb according to whichever shuttle bus is leaving next.

ORIENTATION TO BRÚ NA BÓINNE

Cost: Newgrange—€7, Knowth—€6, both—€13; museum is included in tomb prices.

Hours: Daily 9:00-19:00, slightly shorter hours mid-Sept-May, last entry to visitors center 45 minutes before closing. Newgrange is open year-round, while Knowth is open May-Oct only.

Information: Tel. 041/988-0300, www.heritageireland.ie.

Crowd-Beating Tips: Arrive early—ideally before 9:30 in peak season—to avoid the big midday bus-tour crowds from Dublin. Visits are limited, and on busy summer days those arriving in the afternoon may not get a spot on a shuttle bus. An advance reservation system might be in place by the time you visit (check the website). The last bus to the tombs leaves 1.75 hours before closing.

VISITING BRÚ NA BÓINNE

At the visitors center, buy your ticket (to one or both tombs), find out when the next shuttle bus leaves, then spend your waiting time in the excellent museum, grabbing lunch in the cheery downstairs cafeteria, and using the WCs (there are none at the tomb sites).

Brú na Bóinne Visitors Center Museum

The museum introduces you to the Boyne River Valley and its tombs. No one knows exactly who built the 40 burial mounds found in the surrounding hills. Exhibits re-create what these pre-Celtic people might have been like—simple farmers and hunters living in huts, fishing in the Boyne, equipped with crude tools of stone, bone, or wood.

Then around 3200 b.c., someone had a bold idea. They constructed a chamber of large stones, with a long stone-lined passage leading up to it. They covered it with a huge mound of dirt and rocks in successive layers. Sailing down the Boyne to the sea, they beached at Clogherhead (12.5 miles from here), where they found hundreds of five-ton stones, weathered smooth by the tides. Somehow they transported them back up the Boyne, possibly by tying a raft to the top of the stone so it was lifted free by a high tide. They then hauled these stones up the hill by rolling them atop logs and up dirt ramps, and laid them around the perimeter of the burial mound to hold everything in place. It would have taken anywhere from five years to a generation to construct a single large tomb.

Why build these vast structures? Partially, it was to bury VIPs. A dead king might be carried up the hill to be cremated on a pyre. Then they'd bring his ashes into the tomb, parading by torchlight down the passage to the central chamber. The remains were placed in a ceremonial basin, mingled with those of his illustrious ancestors.

To help bring the history to life, the museum displays replicas of tools and objects found at the sites, including the ceremonial basin stone and a head made from flint, which may have been carried atop a pole during the funeral procession. Marvel at the craftsmanship of the perfectly spherical stones (and the phallic one), and wonder at their purpose.

The tombs also served an astronomical function; they're precisely aligned to the movements of the sun, as displays and a video illustrate. You can request a short tour and winter solstice light-show demo at a full-size replica of the Newgrange passage and interior chamber.

Since the tombs are aligned with the heavens, it begs the question: Were these structures sacred places where primal Homo sapiens gathered to ponder the deepest mysteries of existence?

▲▲▲Newgrange

This grassy mound atop a hill is 250 feet across and 40 feet high. Dating from 3200 B.C., it's 500 years older than the pyramids at Giza. The base of the mound is ringed by dozens of curbstones, each about nine feet long and weighing five tons.

The entrance facade is a mosaic of white quartz and dark granite. This is a reconstruction done in the 1970s, and not every archaeologist agrees it originally looked like this. Above the doorway is a square window called the roofbox, which played a key role (as we'll see). In front of the doorway lies the most famous of the curbstones, the 10- by 4-foot entrance stone. Its left half is carved with three mysterious spirals, which have become a kind of poster child for prehistoric art.

Most of Newgrange's curbstones have designs carved into them. This was done with super-hard flint tools; the Neolithic ("New Stone Age") people had not mastered metal. The stones feature common Neolithic motifs: not people or animals, but geometric shapes—spirals, crosshatches, bull's-eyes, and chevrons.

Entering the tomb, you walk down a narrow 60-foot passage lined with big boulders. Occasionally you have to duck or turn sideways to squeeze through. The passage opens up into a central room—a cross-shaped central chamber with three alcoves, topped by a 20-foot-high igloo-type stone dome. Bones and ashes were placed here in a ceremonial stone basin, under 200,000 tons of stone and dirt.

While we know nothing of Newgrange's builders, it most certainly was a sacred spot—for a cult of the dead, a cult of the sun, or both. The tomb is aligned precisely east-west. As the sun rises around the shortest day of the year (winter solstice—usually on Dec 21—and two days before and after), a ray of light enters through the roofbox and creeps slowly down the passageway. For 17 minutes, it lights the center of the sacred chamber (your guide will demonstrate this). Perhaps this was the moment when the souls of the dead were transported to the afterlife, via that ray of life-giving and life-taking light. Then the light passes on, and, for the next 361 days, the tomb sits again in total darkness.

▲▲▲Knowth

This site is an impressive necropolis, with one grand hill-topping mound surrounded by several smaller satellite tombs. The central mound is 220 feet wide, 40 feet high, and covers 1.5 acres.

You'll see plenty of mysteriously carved curbstones and new-feeling grassy mounds that you can look down on from atop the grand tomb.

Knowth's big tomb has two passages: one entering from the east, and one from the west. Like Newgrange, it's likely aligned so the rising and setting sun shone down the passageways to light the two interior chambers, but these are aligned to the equinox rather than the solstice. Neither passage is open to the public, but you can visit a room carved into the mound by archaeologists, where a cutaway lets you see the layers of dirt and rock used to build the mound. You also get a glimpse down one of the passages.

The Knowth site thrived from 3000 to 2000 B.C. The central tomb dates from about 2000 B.C. It was likely used for burial rituals and sun-tracking ceremonies to please the gods and ensure the regular progression of seasons for crops. The site then evolved into the domain of fairies and myths for the next 2,000 years, and became an Iron Age fortress in the early centuries after Christ. Around A.D. 1000, it was an all-Ireland political center, and later, a Norman fortress was built atop the mound. Now, 4,000 years after prehistoric people built these strange tombs, you can stand atop the hill at Knowth, look out over the surrounding countryside, and contemplate.

More Boyne Valley Sights

▲▲Battle of the Boyne Site

One of Europe's lesser-known battlegrounds (but huge in Irish and British history), this is the pastoral riverside site of the pivotal battle in which the Protestant British decisively broke Catholic resistance, establishing Protestant rule over all of Ireland and Britain.

Cost and Hours: €5, daily 9:00-17:00, Oct-April until 16:00, last entry one hour before closing, tearoom/cafeteria, tel. 041/980-9950, www.battleoftheboyne.ie.

Getting There: The visitors center is on the south bank of the Boyne River, about two miles north of the village of Donore. It's well signposted for drivers from M-1, N-51, or N-2. Once you pass through the main gates, you'll find the visitors center in the mansion a quarter-mile up the driveway.

"Living History" demonstrations: The Sunday afternoon "Living History" demonstrations (March-Sept) are a treat for history buffs and photographers, with guides clad in 17th-century garb. You'll get a bang out of the musket loading and firing demo. Or catch the cavalry combat in full gallop and learn that to be an Irish watermelon is to fear the sword. Check the event program online for schedules and additional offerings such as battlefield walks.

Background: It was here in 1690 that Protestant King William III, with his English/Irish/Dutch/Danish/French Huguenot army, defeated his father-in-law—who was also his uncle—Catholic King James II and his Irish/French army. At stake was who would sit on the British throne, who would hold religious power in Ireland, and whether or not French dominance of Europe would continue.

King William's forces, on the north side of the Boyne, managed to fight their way across the river, and by the end of the day, King James was fleeing south in full retreat. He soon left Ireland, but his forces fought on until their final defeat a year later. James II (called "James da Turd" by those who scorn his lack of courage and leadership) never returned, and he died a bitter ex-monarch in France. His "Jacobite" claim to the English throne lived on among Catholics for decades, and was finally extinguished in 1745, when his grandson, Bonnie Prince Charlie, was defeated at the Battle of Culloden in Scotland.

King William of Orange's victory, on the other hand, is still celebrated in Northern Ireland every July 12, with controversial marches by Unionist "Orangemen." The battle actually took place on July 1, but was officially shifted 11 days later when the Gregorian calendar was adopted in 1752. (Even the calendar has been affected by religious strife: Protestant nations were reluctant to use a calendar developed by a Catholic—Pope Gregory in 1582. So England delayed adoption of Gregory's calendar for 170 years.)

The 60,000 soldiers who fought here made this one of the largest battles ever to take place in the British Isles. Yet it was only a side skirmish in an even larger continental confrontation pitting France's King Louis XIV against the "Grand Alliance" of nations threatened by France's mighty military and frequent incursions into neighboring lands.

Louis ruled by divine right, answerable only to God—and James modeled himself after Louis. Even the pope (who could control neither Louis nor James and was equally disturbed by Catholic France's aggressions) backed Protestant King William against

Catholic King James—just one example of the pretzel logic that was the European mindset at the time.

The site of the Battle of the Boyne was bought in 1997 by the Irish Office of Public Works, part of the Republic's governmental efforts to respect a place sacred to Unionists in Northern Ireland—despite the fact that the battle's outcome ensured Catholic subordination to the Protestant minority for the next 230 years.

Visiting the Site: The **visitors center** is housed in a mansion built on the battlefield 50 years after the conflict. The exhibits do a good job of illustrating the international nature of the battle and its place in the wider context of European political power struggles. The highlight is a huge battleground model with laser lights that move troops around the terrain, showing the battle's ebb and flow on that bloody day. A separate 15-minute film (shown in the former stable house) runs continuously and does a fine job of fleshing out the battle.

As you exit the site to the north (on the L-16014 access road that connects to the main N-51 road), you'll cross the River Boyne on a **metal bridge,** locally referred to as "Old Bridge." This spot is where the most frantic action took place on that bloody day.

Pull over and gaze down at the river. Picture crack Dutch troops (from King William's homeland) marching south in formation. They were the first to cross the river here, while their comrades behind on the north bank covered their exposed position with constant protective fire. Low tides (the sea is only 7 miles downstream) allowed these soldiers to cross the river in water up to their waists. Between the gun smoke, weapon fire, and shouts filling the air, it was tough to tell friend from foe in the close, chaotic combat. Neither force had standard uniforms, so King William's troops wore sprigs of green while the troops of King James pinned white paper to their coats. Both sides bled red.

▲Hill of Tara

This site was the most important center of political and religious power in pre-Christian Ireland. While aerial views show plenty of mystifying circles and lines, wandering with the sheep among the well-worn ditches and hills leaves you with more to feel than to see. Visits are made meaningful by an excellent 20-minute video presentation and the insightful 20-minute guided walk that usually follows (walk times unpredictable due to frequent big bus tours; worth calling ahead to confirm availability). Wear good walking shoes—the ground is uneven and often wet.

Cost and Hours: €5, includes video and guided walk (if available when you visit), buy tickets from old church in the trees above parking lot; daily 10:00-18:00, last tour at 17:00, from mid-Sept-mid-May access is free but visitors center is closed; WCs in café next to parking lot, tel. 046/902-5903, http://hilloftara.org.

Visiting the Site: You'll see the Mound of Hostages (a Bronze Age passage grave, c. 2500 B.C.), a couple of ancient sacred stones, a war memorial, and vast views over the Emerald Isle. While ancient Ireland was a pig pile of minor chieftain-kings scrambling for power, the high king of Tara was king of the mountain. It was at this ancient stockade that St. Patrick directly challenged the king's authority. When confronted by the high king, Patrick convincingly explained the Holy Trinity using a shamrock: three petals with one stem. He won the right to preach Christianity throughout Ireland, and the country had a new national symbol.

This now-desolate hill was also the scene of great modern events. In 1798, passionate young Irish rebels chose Tara for its defensible position, but were routed by better organized (and more sober) British troops. (The cunning British commander had sent three cartloads of whiskey along the nearby road earlier in the day, knowing the rebels would intercept it.) In 1843, the great orator and champion of Irish liberty Daniel O'Connell gathered 500,000 Irish peasants on this hill for his greatest "monster meeting"—a peaceful show of force demanding the repeal of the Act of Union with Britain (kind of the Woodstock of its day). In a bizarre final twist, a small group of British Israelites—who believed they were one of the lost tribes of Israel, who had ended up in Britain—spent 1899 to 1901 recklessly digging up parts of the hill in a misguided search for the Ark of the Covenant.

Stand on the Hill of Tara. Think of the history it's seen, and survey Ireland. It's understandable why this "meeting place of heroes" continues to hold a powerful place in the Irish psyche.

Old Mellifont Abbey

This Cistercian abbey (the first in Ireland) was established by French monks who came to the country in 1142 to bring the Irish monks more in line with Rome. (Even the abbey's architecture was unusual, marking the first time in Ireland that a formal, European-style monastic layout was used.) Cistercians lived isolated rural lives; lay monks worked the land, allowing the more educated monks to devote all their energy to prayer. After Henry VIII dissolved the abbey in 1539, centuries of locals used it as a handy quarry. Consequently, little survives beyond the octagonal lavabo, where the monks would ceremonially wash their hands before entering the refectory to eat. The lavabo gives a sense of the abbey's former grandeur.

The excellent 45-minute tours, available upon request and included in your admission (late May-Aug only), give meaning to what you're seeing. To get a better idea of the extent of the site, check out the model of the monastery in its heyday, located at the back of the small museum next to the ticket desk.

Cost and Hours: €5; daily 10:00-18:00, last tour at 17:30, last entry 45 minutes before closing; from Sept-late May site is free but there are no tours; tel. 041/988-0300, www.heritageireland.ie.

Monasterboice

This ruined monastery is visit-worthy for its round tower and its ornately carved high crosses—two of the best such crosses in Ireland. In the Dark Ages, these crosses, illustrated from top to bottom with Bible stories, gave monks a teaching tool as they preached to the illiterate masses. Imagine the crosses in their prime, when they were brightly painted (before years of wind and rain weathered the paint away). Today, Monasterboice is basically an old graveyard.

Cost and Hours: Free and always open.

Visiting the Site: The 18-foot-tall **Cross of Murdock** (Muiredach's Cross, c. 923, named after an abbot) is considered the best high cross in Ireland. The circle—which characterizes the Irish high cross—could represent the perfection of God. Or, to help ease pagans into Christianity, it may represent the sun, which was worshipped in pre-Christian Celtic society. Whatever its symbolic purpose, its practical function was to support the weight of the crossbeam.

Face the cross (with the round tower in the background) and study the carved sandstone. The center panel shows the Last

Judgment, with Christ under a dove, symbolizing the Holy Spirit. Those going to heaven are on Christ's right, and the damned are being ushered away by a pitchfork-wielding devil on his left. Working down, you'll see the Archangel Michael weighing souls, as the Devil tugs demonically at the scales; the adoration of the three—or four—Magi; Moses striking the rock to bring forth water; scenes from the life of David; and, finally, Adam, Eve, and the apple next to Cain slaying Abel. Imagine these carvings with their original, colorful paint jobs. Check out the plaque at the base of the nearby tree, which further explains the carvings on the cross.

Find the even taller cross nearest the tower. It seems the top section was broken off and buried for a period, which protected it from weathering. The bottom part remained standing, enduring the erosive effect of Irish weather, which smeared the once-crisp features.

The door to the round tower was originally 15-20 feet above the ground (accessible by ladder). After centuries of burials, the ground level has risen.

Trim

The sleepy, workaday town of Trim, straddling the River Boyne, is marked by the towering ruins of Trim Castle. Trim feels littered with mighty ruins that seem to say, "This little town was big-time...800 years ago." The tall Yellow Steeple (over the river from the castle) is all that remains of the 14th-century Augustinian Abbey of St. Mary. Not far away, the Sheep's Gate is a humble remnant of the once-grand medieval town walls. Near the town center, the modest, 30-foot-tall Wellington Column honors native son Arthur Wellesley, the First Duke of Wellington (1769-1852), who spent his childhood in Trim, defeated Napoleon at Waterloo, and twice became prime minister.

Trim makes a great landing pad into—or launching pad out of—Ireland. If you're flying into or out of Dublin Airport and don't want to deal with big-city Dublin, this is a perfect alternative—an easy 45-minute, 30-mile drive away. You can rent a car at the airport and make Trim your first overnight base (getting used to driving on the other side of the road in easier country traffic). Or spend your last night here before returning your car at the airport. Weather permitting, my evening stroll makes for a fine first or last night in the Emerald Isle.

Orientation to Trim

Trim's main square is a traffic roundabout, and everything's within a block or two. Most of the shops and eateries are on or near Market Street, along with banks and a supermarket.

TOURIST INFORMATION

The TI is right next to the castle entrance and includes a handy coffee shop. Drop in to pick up a free map (Mon-Fri 9:30-17:30, Sat-Sun 12:00-17:00, shorter hours Sept-May, Castle Street, tel. 046/943-7227). Outside, 100 feet to the right of the TI door, you'll find a plaque with photos showing the castle dolled up for the filming of *Braveheart*.

HELPFUL HINTS

Laundry: The launderette is located close to Market Street (Mon-Sat 9:00-13:00 & 13:30-17:30, closed Sun, Watergate Street, tel. 046/943-7176).

Parking: To park on the street or in a public lot, use the pay-and-display parking system (€1/hour, 2-hour maximum, Mon-Sat 9:00-18:00, free Sun).

Taxi: Donie Quinn can give you a lift to nearby Boyne sites (tel. 046/943-6009).

Adventure Tours: Boyne Valley Activities offers kayaking, rafting, high-rope walks, and archery excursions...luckily not simultaneously (€25 for archery; €40 for rafting, kayaking, and high-rope walks; call ahead to reserve, mobile 086-734-2585, www.boynevalleyactivities.ie).

Marc O'Regan leads backcountry trout and pike fishing tours, making a splash with anglers who want to experience Ireland's bountiful lakes and rivers (tel. 046/943-1635, www.crannmor.com). O'Regan and his wife also run the recommended Crannmór Guest House.

Sights in Trim

▲▲Trim Castle

This is the biggest Norman castle in Ireland. Set in a grassy riverside park at the edge of this sleepy town, its mighty keep tow-

ers above a very ruined outer wall. It replaced a wooden fortification that was destroyed in 1173 by Irish High King Rory O'Connor, who led a raid against the invading Normans. The current castle was completed in the 1220s and served as a powerful Norman statement to the restless Irish natives. It remained a

sharp barb at the fringe of "the Pale" (English-controlled territory), when English rule shrank to just the area around Dublin in the 1400s. By that time, any lands farther west were "beyond the Pale."

Cost and Hours: €5 for entrance to keep and required tour, €2 for gardens only; daily 10:00-18:00, Nov-mid-March open Sat-Sun only 10:00-17:00, last entry one hour before closing, 45-minute tours run 2/hour but spots are limited and can fill up—so arrive early in peak season, tel. 046/943-8619, www.heritageireland.ie.

Visiting the Castle: Today the castle remains an impressive sight—so impressive that it was used in the 1994 filming of *Braveheart* (which was actually about Scotland's—not Ireland's—fight

NEAR DUBLIN

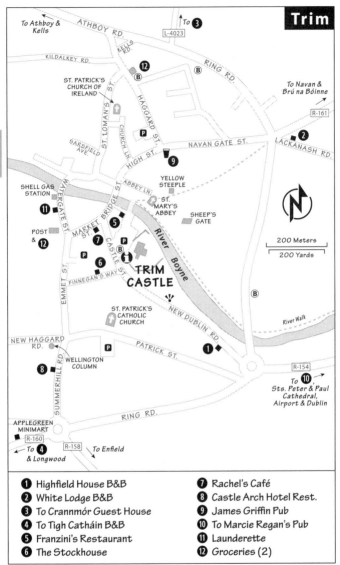

To Athboy & Kells
ATHBOY RD.
↑ To ③
L-4023
KILDALKEY RD.
KELLS RD.
RING RD.
To Navan & Brú na Bóinne
R-161
ST. PATRICK'S CHURCH OF IRELAND
ST. LOMAN'S ST.
CHURCH LN.
HAGGARD ST.
⑫ Ⓑ
Ⓑ
P
NAVAN GATE ST.
LACKANASH RD.
② ❷
SARSFIELD AVE.
HIGH ST.
⑨
YELLOW STEEPLE
ST. MARY'S ABBEY
ABBEY LN.
SHEEP'S GATE
River Boyne
SHELL GAS STATION
⑪
WATERGATE ST.
MARKET ST.
BRIDGE ST.
⑤
Ⓑ
CASTLE ST.
P
❶
POST &
⑫
EMMET ST.
⑦
P
⑥
FINNEGAN'S WAY
TRIM CASTLE
N
200 Meters
200 Yards
ST. PATRICK'S CATHOLIC CHURCH
NEW DUBLIN RD.
Ⓑ
River Walk
NEW HAGGARD RD.
SUMMERHILL RD.
P
WELLINGTON COLUMN
PATRICK ST.
⬥ ❶
R-154
⑧
To ⑩ Sts. Peter & Paul Cathedral, Airport & Dublin
RING RD.
APPLEGREEN MINIMART
R-160
← To ④ & Longwood
R-158
To Enfield

Trim

① Highfield House B&B
② White Lodge B&B
③ To Crannmór Guest House
④ To Tigh Catháin B&B
⑤ Franzini's Restaurant
⑥ The Stockhouse
⑦ Rachel's Café
⑧ Castle Arch Hotel Rest.
⑨ James Griffin Pub
⑩ To Marcie Regan's Pub
⑪ Launderette
⑫ Groceries (2)

for freedom from the English). The best-preserved walls ring the castle's southern perimeter and sport a barbican gate that contained two drawbridges.

At the base of the castle walls, notice the cleverly angled "batter" wall—used by defenders who hurled down stones that banked off at great velocity into the attacking army. Notice also that the castle is built directly on bedrock, visible along the base of the walls. During sieges, while defenders of other castles feared that attackers would tunnel underground to weaken the defensive walls, that was not an issue here.

The massive 70-foot-high central keep, which is mostly a hollow shell, has 20 sides. This experimental design was not implemented elsewhere because it increased the number of defenders needed to cover all the angles. You can go inside the keep only with the included tour, where you'll start by checking out the cool ground-floor models showing the evolution of the castle. Then you'll climb a series of tightly winding original staircases and modern, high catwalks, learn about life in the castle, and end at the top with great views of the walls and the countryside.

Make time to take a 15-minute walk outside, circling the castle walls and stopping at the informative plaques that show the castle from each viewpoint during its gory glory days. Night strollers are treated to views of the castle hauntingly lit in blue-green hues.

NEAR DUBLIN

Trim Evening Stroll

Given good weather, here's my blueprint for a fine night in Trim. Start the evening by taking the pleasant **River Walk** stroll along the River Boyne from Trim Castle. Cross the wooden footbridge over the river behind the castle and turn right (east). The paved, level trail eventually leads under a modern bridge/overpass and extends a mile along fields that serfs farmed 750 years ago. During the filming of *Braveheart*, Mel Gibson's character met the French princess in her tent in these fields, with the castle looming in the background.

The trail ends in the medieval ruins of **Newtown.** This was indeed once the "new town" (mid-1200s) that sprouted as a religious satellite community to support the political power housed in the castle. Wander the sprawling, ragtag ruins of **Saints Peter and Paul Cathedral** (1206), once the largest Gothic church in Ireland. Seek out the tomb with a carved lid depicting a medieval lord and lady; this is known locally as the tomb of the "jealous man and woman" (because they do not touch each other). Upon close inspection, you'll notice hundreds of tiny pins in the creases of the carving, left behind by superstitious visitors. Why? If you rub a pin on your stubborn wart and then leave it here...presto: wart-be-gone.

Just beyond the ruins, cross the old Norman bridge to the 13th-century scraps of the **Hospital of St. John the Baptist.** Medieval medicine couldn't have been fun, but this hospital was the best you could hope for back when life was nasty, brutish, and short. Many a knight was spent here.

Cross back over the bridge and stop for a pint at tiny, atmospheric **Marcie Regan's,** one of the oldest pubs in Ireland (an exterior sign calls it "Regan's," but most locals call it "Marcie's"). Explore its dimly lit back rooms. The pub sits beside one of the oldest bridges in Ireland (the one you just crossed).

Then walk back along the river the way you came and have dinner at the recommended **Franzini's** restaurant beside the castle. After dinner, assist your digestion by walking a lap around the castle (beautifully lit at night). End the evening a few blocks away with a pint at the recommended **James Griffin** pub. A fine night 'tis...or 'twas.

Sleeping in Trim

Because Trim is a popular spot for weddings, book as early as possible if you are visiting on a summer weekend.

$$ Highfield House B&B, across the street from the castle and a five-minute walk from town, is a stately 210-year-old former maternity hospital, with hardwood floors and 10 spacious, high-ceilinged rooms (family rooms; above the roundabout where Dublin Road hits Trim, just before castle at Castle Street; tel. 046/943-6386, mobile 086-857-7115, www.highfieldguesthouse.com, info@highfieldguesthouse.com, Geraldine and Edward Duignan).

$ White Lodge B&B, a 10-minute walk northeast of the castle, has six comfortably unpretentious rooms with an oak-and-granite lounge (open May-Oct, family room, parking, New Road, tel. 046/943-6549, www.whitelodge.ie, info@whitelodge.ie, Todd O'Loughlin). They also offer a family-friendly self-catering house next door. A handy 300-yard trail leads from across the street to the castle.

Countryside B&Bs: These two B&Bs are in the quiet countryside about a mile outside Trim (phone ahead for driving directions).

At ivy-draped **$ Crannmór Guest House,** Anne O'Regan decorates five rooms with cheery color schemes (family room; north of the Ring Road on Dunderry Road L-4023, then veer right at the first fork; tel. 046/943-1635, mobile 087-288-7390, www.crannmor.com, cranmor@eircom.net). Anne's professional-guide husband Marc knows all the best fishing holes (listed earlier, under "Helpful Hints").

Marie Keane's **$ Tigh Catháin B&B,** southwest of town, has four large, bright, lacy rooms with a comfy, rural feel and organically grown produce at breakfast (cash only, on R-160/Longwood Road, 200 yards past the Applegreen minimart, tel. 046/943-1996, mobile 086-257-7313, www.tighcathain-bnb.com, tighcathain.bnb@gmail.com).

Eating in Trim

A country market town, Trim offers basic meat-and-potatoes lunch and dinner options. My first two listings are really the only full restaurants in town. Otherwise, the spots along Market Street are friendly, wholesome, and unassuming.

$$$ Franzini's has a fun dinner menu and an excellent location next to the castle. They serve pasta, steak, fish, and great salads in a modern, plush space (Mon-Sat 17:00-21:00, Sun 14:00-20:00, on French's Lane across from the castle parking lot, tel. 046/943-1002).

$$$ The Stockhouse serves hearty steaks and poultry, plus creative desserts. Sit upstairs and take in the history of Trim from the walls while you wait (Mon-Thu 17:00-21:00, Fri-Sat until 22:00, Sun 13:00-20:30, Finnegan's Way, tel. 046/943-7388).

$$ Rachel's Café is a good bet along Market Street for salads, sandwiches, and meat pies (Mon-Sat 8:30-17:30, Sun until 17:00, tel. 046/943-1636).

The **$$ Castle Arch Hotel,** popular with locals, serves hearty pub grub at reasonable prices in its bistro on Summerhill Road (daily 12:30-21:00, tel. 046/943-1516).

Pubs: For a fun pub experience, check out Trim's two best watering holes. The **James Griffin** (on High Street) is full of local characters with traditional Irish music sessions on Monday, Wednesday, and Thursday nights. Locals fill the tiny, low-ceilinged **Marcie Regan's,** a creaky, unpretentious pub at the north end of the old Norman bridge over the River Boyne—it's a half-mile stroll outside town, next to the ruins of Newtown.

Supermarkets: Several stores offer picnic supplies. These include **Spar Market** (Mon-Sat 7:30-20:00, Sun 8:30-19:00, Emmett Street) and the larger **Super Valu** (daily 8:00-22:00, on Haggard Street, a bit farther from the town center).

Trim Connections

Trim has no train station; the nearest is in Drogheda, 25 miles away on the coast. Buses from Trim to **Dublin** (almost hourly, 1 hour) pick you up at the bus shelter next to the TI and castle entrance on Castle Street. For details, see www.buseireann.ie.

Glendalough and the Wicklow Mountains

The Wicklow Mountains, while only 15 miles south of Dublin, feel remote—enough so to have provided a handy refuge for opponents to English rule. Rebels who took part in the 1798 Irish uprising hid out here for years. The area only became more accessible in 1800, when the frustrated British built a military road to help flush out the rebels. Today, this same road—now R-115—takes you through the Wicklow area to Glendalough at its south end. While the valley is the darling of Dublin day-trip tour organizers, for the most part it doesn't live up to the hype. But two blockbuster sights—Glendalough and the Powerscourt Estate Gardens—make a visit worth considering.

GETTING AROUND THE WICKLOW AREA

By car or tour, it's easy. If you lack wheels, take a tour. It's not worth the trouble on public transport.

By Car

It's a delight. Take N-11 south from Dublin toward Bray, then R-117 to Enniskerry, the gateway to the Wicklow Mountains. Signs direct you to the gardens and on to Glendalough. From Glendalough, if you're heading west, you can leave the valley (and pick up the highway to the west) over the famous but dull mountain pass called the Wicklow Gap.

By Tour from Dublin

Bus Tours: Several companies offer tours around the region. **Wild Wicklow Tours** gives you an entertaining guide who packs every minute of an all-day excursion with information and *craic* (interesting, fun conversation). With a gang of 40 packed into tight but comfortable, mountain-gripping buses, the guide kicks into gear from the first pickup in Dublin. Tours cover the windy military road over scenic Sally Gap and the Glendalough monasteries (€28, ask for discount with this book, runs daily year-round, stop for lunch at a pub—cost not included, several Dublin hotel pickup points, return to Dublin by 18:00, advance booking required, tel. 01/280-1899, www.wildwicklow.ie).

Do Dublin Tours offers a shorter trip focusing on Wicklow's two main sights, Glendalough and Powerscourt Gardens, aboard bright-green, double-decker buses (€22, daily departure at 10:30,

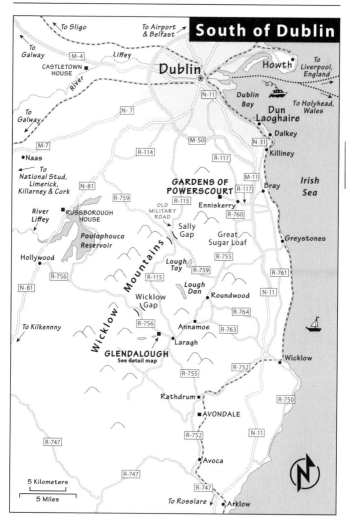

return by 17:00, tours depart from Dublin Bus head office, 59 Upper O'Connell Street, tel. 01/844-4265, www.dodublin.ie).

Local Guide: Friendly and knowledgeable **Lisa Tully** knows the region and can show you the worthwhile stops on your drives around County Wicklow (when she's not on the road leading Rick Steves tours). If you're without a car, she also offers scenic walking tours—meet her by train from Dublin or she'll arrange a driver to get you to and from the countryside (€40/hour, available March-Nov, tel. 086/898-6457, www.wicklowguidedtours.ie, lisa@wicklowguidedtours.ie).

Sights in the Wicklow Area

▲▲Powerscourt Estate Gardens

A mile above the village of Enniskerry, the Powerscourt Estate Gardens cover 47 acres within a 700-acre estate. The dreamy driveway alone is a mile long. The mansion's interior is only partially restored after a 1974 fire (and only available for special events). But its meticulously kept aristocratic gardens are Ireland's best. The house was commissioned in the 1730s by Richard Wingfield, first viscount of Powerscourt. The gardens you see today were created during the Victorian era (1858-1875).

Upon entry, you'll get a flier laying out 40-minute and one-hour walks. The "one-hour" walk takes 30 minutes at a relaxed amble. With the impressive summit of the Great Sugar Loaf Mountain as a backdrop, and a fine Japanese garden, Italian garden, and goofy pet cemetery along the way, this attraction provides the scenic greenery I hoped to find in the rest of the Wicklow area. Parts of the lush movies *Barry Lyndon* and *The Count of Monte Cristo* were filmed in this well-watered aristocratic fantasy.

Spend 10 minutes checking out the easy-to-miss film room, which provides a history of the estate and a model of Powerscourt House before the fire.

Cost and Hours: €10, daily 9:30-17:30, Nov-Feb until dusk, great cafeteria, tel. 01/204-6000, www.powerscourt.com.

Other Sights: Kids may enjoy a peek at the antique dollhouses of the upstairs **Tara's Palace Museum of Childhood** (€5, proceeds go to children's charities, Mon-Sat 10:00-17:00, Sun from 12:00). Skip the Powerscourt Waterfall (4 miles away).

▲Old Military Road over Sally Gap

This trip is only for those with a car. From the Powerscourt Gardens and Enniskerry, go to Glencree, where you drive the tiny old military road (R-115) over Sally Gap and through the best scenery of the Wicklow Mountains (on Sundays, watch for dozens of bicycle racers). Look for the German military cemetery, built for U-boat sailors who washed ashore in World War II. Near Sally Gap, notice the peat bogs and the freshly cut peat bricks drying in the wind. Many locals are nostalgic for the "good old days," when homes were always peat-fire heated. At the Sally Gap junction, turn left, where a road winds through the vast Guinness estate. Look down on the glacial lake (Lough Tay) nicknamed "Guinness Lake," as the water looks like Ireland's favorite dark-brown stout, and the sand of the beach actually looks like the head of a Guinness

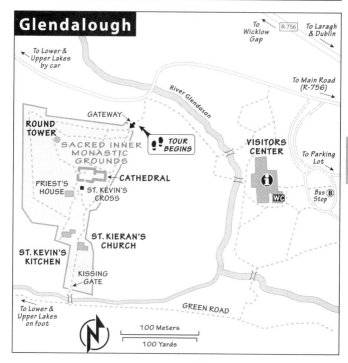

beer. The History Channel series *Vikings* was primarily filmed on a temporary set built on the shores of the lake. From here, the road meanders scenically down into the village of Roundwood and on to Glendalough.

▲▲Glendalough

The steep wooded slopes of Glendalough (GLEN-da-lock, "Valley of the Two Lakes"), at the south end of Wicklow's old military road, hide Ireland's most impressive monastic settlement. Founded by St. Kevin in the sixth century, the monastery flourished (despite repeated Viking raids) throughout the Age of Saints and Scholars until the English destroyed it in 1398. A few hardy holy men continued to live here until it was finally abandoned during the Dissolution of the Monasteries in 1539. But pilgrims kept coming, especially on St. Kevin's Day, June 3. (This might have something to do with the fact that a pope said seven visits to Glendalough had the same indulgence—or forgiveness from sins—value as one visit to Rome.) While much restoration was done in the 1870s, most of the buildings date from the 10th to 12th century.

In an Ireland without cities, these monastic communities were mainstays of civilization. At such remote outposts, ascetics (with a taste for scenic settings, but abstaining from worldly pleasures) gathered to commune with God. In the 12th century, with the arrival of grander monastic orders such as the Cistercians, Benedictines, Augustinians, Franciscans, and Dominicans, and with the growth of cities, these monastic communities were eclipsed. Today, Ireland is dotted with the reminders of this age: illuminated manuscripts, simple churches, carved crosses, and about 100 round towers.

The valley sights are split between the two lakes. The smaller, lower lake is just beyond the visitors center and nearer the best remaining ruins. The upper lake has scant ruins and feels like a state park, with a grassy lakeside picnic area and school groups. Walkers and hikers will enjoy a choice of nine different trails of varying lengths through the lush Wicklow countryside (longest loop takes four hours, hiking-trail maps available at visitors center).

Planning Your Time: Summer tour-bus crowds are terrible all day on weekends and 11:00-14:00 on weekdays. If you're there at midday, your best bet is to take the once-daily, 45-minute tour of the site (June-Aug only at 13:30, departs from visitors center). Otherwise, ask if you can tag along with a prebooked tour group's tour. If you're on your own, find the markers that give short descriptions of the ruined buildings.

Here's a good day-plan: Park for free at the visitors center. Visit the center; take the guided tour if possible; wander the ruins surrounding the round tower on your own (free); or walk the traffic-free Green Road a half-mile to the upper lake, and then walk back to the visitors center and your car along the trail that parallels the public road (an easy, roughly one-mile loop). Or you can drive to the upper lake. If you're rushed, skip the upper lake.

Cost and Hours: Free to enter site, €5 for visitors center, €4 to park at upper lake; open daily 9:30-18:00, mid-Oct-mid-March until 17:00; last entry 45 minutes before closing, tel. 0404/45352.

Visiting Glendalough: Start out at the **Glendalough Visitors Centre,** where a 15-minute video provides a good thumbnail background on monastic society in medieval Ireland. While the video is more general than specific to Glendalough, the adjacent museum room does feature this particular monastic settlement. The model in the center of the room re-creates the fortified village of the year 1050. Interactive exhibits show the contributions these monks made to intellectual life in Dark Age Europe (such as illuminated manuscripts and Irish minuscule, a more compact alphabet developed in the seventh century).

When you're ready to visit the site, head out behind the visitors center, cross the bridge over the brook, and follow the lane 100 yards to the original stone **gateway.** From here you enter the sacred inner-monastic grounds that provided sanctuary for anyone under threat. Look for the cross carved into the sanctuary stone in the gateway (at knee level). A refugee had 90 days to live safely within the walls. But on the 91st day, he would be tossed out to the waiting authorities...unless he became a monk (in which case he could live there indefinitely, no matter what his crime).

The graceful **round tower** rises from an evocative tangle of tombstones. Easily the best ruins of Glendalough gather within 100 yards of this famous 110-foot-tall tower. Towers like this (usually 60-110 feet tall with windows facing the four cardinal compass points) were standard features in such monastic settlements. They functioned as bell towers, storage lofts, beacons for pilgrims, and last-resort refuges during Viking raids. (But given enough warning, monks were safer hiding in the surrounding forest.) The towers had a high door with a pull-up ladder—both for safety and because a door at ground level would have weak-ened the tower's foundation. Several ruined churches (10th-12th century) lurk nearby...seek them out.

The **cathedral** is the largest and most central of all the ruins. It evolved over time with various expansions and through the reuse of stones from previous structures. The larger nave came first, and the chancel (up the couple of stairs where the altar later stood) was an addition. The east window faces toward Jerusalem and the rising sun, symbolic of Christ rising from the dead. Under the southern window is a small wall cupboard with a built-in basin. The holy vessels used during Mass were rinsed here so that the holy sacra-mental water would drain directly into the ground, avoiding any contamination (look for the tiny drain in the center).

Nearby is **St. Kevin's Cross.** At 10 feet tall and carved from a single block of granite, this cross was a statement of utter devo-tion. (Most other famous Irish high crosses were carved of softer sandstone, allowing their carvers to create more ornate depictions of biblical stories than you'll see here.) According to legend, if you hug this cross and can reach your hands around to touch your fin-gers on the other side, you'll have your wish granted (and your jeal-ous friends labeling you a knuckle dragger). St. Kevin: the patron saint of dislocated shoulders.

Heading downhill, you'll pass the tiny **priests' house,** which was completely reconstructed (using the original stones) from a 1779 sketch. It might have originally acted as a kind of treasury, housing the relics of St. Kevin.

Farther down, you'll come to perhaps the prettiest structure surviving on the site: **St. Kevin's "kitchen"** (actually a church).

Its short round tower appeared to earlier visitors to be a chimney, but its function was always as a belfry. The steeply stacked stone roof conceals a croft (upper story) perhaps used as a scriptorium for copying holy manuscripts. Nearby is the less impressive stone footprint of **St. Kieran's Church,** possibly dedicated to the saint and contemporary of St. Kevin who founded Clonmacnoise Monastery (another scenic sanctuary, on the banks of the River Shannon south of the town of Athlone).

From here, pass through the kissing gate and cross the bridge over the brook. On the other side, if you're short of time, turn left to go back to the visitors center and parking lot. With more time, turn right and explore the lovely tree-shrouded **Green Road,** which leads past the **lower lake** for a half-mile to the **upper lake** as part of a pleasant one-mile loop.

The oldest ruins—scant and hard to find—lie near the upper lake. **St. Kevin's bed** is a cave where the holy hermit-founder of the monastery took shelter. It lies above the left (southern) shore and is visible and reachable only by boat. The story goes that St. Kevin's devotion was so strong that he would strip off his clothes and jump into thorn bushes rather than submit to the pleasures of the flesh. Another tale has him standing in pious stillness with arms outstretched while a bird builds its nest in his hand. If you want a scenic Wicklow walk, begin here.

Avondale House

Located in south County Wicklow (known as the Garden County), this mansion is the birthplace and lifelong home of Charles Stewart Parnell, the Nationalist politician and dynamo often called the "uncrowned King of Ireland."

Cost and Hours: €7, Thu-Sun 11:00-17:00, closed Mon-Wed and all of Nov-Easter, café, tel. 0404/46111, www.heritageisland. com.

Getting There: It's best to visit by car, as Avondale House is too far for the Dublin day-tour buses (45 miles south of Dublin). In good weather, avoid the €5 parking fee by leaving your car along the road (R-752) just outside the estate gate and walking 200 yards to the house. You can also take a train from Dublin's Connolly station to Rathdrum (4/day, 1.5 hours). From there, Avondale is a short taxi ride away (1.5 miles south of town; try Aughrim Cabs—mobile 086-852-5553).

Visiting the House: Upon entering the opulent Georgian "big house" (built in 1777), you'll first view an informative 20-minute video on Parnell's life. Then you're set free to roam with a handout outlining each room's highlights. A fine portrait of Parnell graces the grand, high-ceilinged entry hall, and a painting of his American grandfather, who manned the USS *Constitution* in the War of

1812, hangs in one room. The dining room is all class, with fine plasterwork and hardwood floors. Original furniture, such as Parnell's sturdy canopied bed, graces the remaining rooms, many of which come with cozy fireplaces and views. The lush surrounding estate of over 500 acres, laced with pleasant walking trails, was used by the Irish Forestry Service (Coillte) to try out forestry methods.

Irish National Stud

Ireland's famed County Kildare—just west of Dublin—has long been known to offer the perfect conditions for breeding horses. Its reputation dates all the way back to the 1300s, when Norman war horses were bred here. Kildare's grasslands lie on a bedrock table of limestone, infusing the soil with just the right mix of nutrients for grazing horses. And the nearby River Tully sparkles with high levels of calcium carbonate, essential for building strong bones in the expensive thoroughbreds (some owned by Arab sheikhs) raised and raced here.

In 1900, Colonel William Hall-Walker (Scottish heir to the Johnny Walker distilling fortune) bought a farm on the River Tully and began breeding a line of champion thoroughbreds. His amazing successes and bizarre methods were the talk of the sport. In 1916, the colonel donated his land and horse farm to the British government, which continued breeding horses here. The farm was eventually handed over to the Irish government, which in 1945 created the Irish National Stud Company to promote the thoroughbred industry.

Today, a guided tour of the grounds at the Irish National Stud gives you a fuller appreciation for the amazing horses that call this place home. Animal lovers and horse-racing fans driving between Dublin and Galway can enjoy a couple of hours here, combining the tour with a stroll through the gardens.

GETTING THERE

From M-7, **drivers** take exit #13 and follow the signs five minutes south (don't take exit #12 for the Curragh Racecourse). **Trains** departing Dublin's Heuston station stop at Kildare town (1-3/hour, 45 minutes). A shuttle bus runs from Kildare's train station to the National Stud (2/hour), or you can take a taxi (about €12-15). One **bus** departs Dublin's Busáras station Monday through Saturday at 9:30 and returns from the National Stud at 15:45. On Sunday, two buses run, departing Busáras at 10:00 and 12:00, with returns at 15:00 and 17:30. Confirm this schedule at the Dublin bus station.

NEAR DUBLIN

When Irish Horses Are Running

Every Irish town seems to have a betting shop for passionate locals who love to closely follow (and wager on) their favorite horses. A quick glance at the weekend sports sections of any Irish newspaper gives you an idea of this sport's high profile. Towns from Galway to Dingle host annual horse races that draw rabid fans from all over. Interestingly, Irish horse races run the track clockwise (the opposite direction from races in the US).

The five most prestigious Irish races take place at the **Curragh Racecourse,** just south of Kildare town (March-Oct, 1 hour west of Dublin, 10 minutes from the National Stud, www.curragh.ie). Horses have been raced here since 1741. The broad, open fields nearby are where the battle scenes in *Braveheart* were filmed (the neighboring Irish army base provided the blue-face-painted extras).

ORIENTATION TO IRISH NATIONAL STUD

Cost: €12.50 includes guided tour, plus entry to Japanese Gardens, St. Fiachra's Garden, and Horse Museum.

Hours: Daily 9:00-18:00, closed Nov-Jan, last entry one hour before closing, 30-minute tours depart at 10:30, 12:00, 14:00, and 16:00, tel. 045/521-617, www.irishnationalstud.ie.

Eating: There's a decent cafeteria, or bring your own food and eat at a picnic table by the parking lot.

VISITING IRISH NATIONAL STUD

The guided tour begins in the **Sun Chariot Yard** (named for the winner of the 1942 Fillies Triple Crown), surrounded by stables housing pregnant mares. A 15-minute film of a foal's birth runs continuously in a stall in the corner of the yard.

The adjacent **Foaling Unit** is where births take place, usually from February through May. The gestation period for horses is 11 months, with 90 percent of foals born at night. (In the wild, a mare and her foal born during the day would have been vulnerable to predators as the herd moved on. Instead, horses have adapted so that foals are born at night—and are able to keep up with the herd within a few hours.) Eccentric Colonel Hall-Walker noted the position of the moon and stars at the time of each foal's birth, and sold those born under inauspicious astrological signs (regardless of their parents' stellar racing records).

From here, you'll pass a working saddle-making shop and a forge where horseshoes are still hammered out on an anvil.

At the **Stallion Boxes,** you'll learn how stargazing Colonel Hall-Walker installed skylights in the stables—allowing the heavens maximum influence over the destiny of his prized animals. A brass plaque on the door of each stall proudly states the horse's name and its racing credentials. One stall bears the simple word, "Teaser." The unlucky occupant's job is to identify mares in heat... but rarely is the frustrated stallion given the opportunity to breed. Bummer.

After the tour, meander down the pleasant tree-lined **Tully Walk,** with paddocks on each side. You'll see mares and foals running free, with the occasional cow thrown in for good measure (cattle have a calming effect on rowdy horses). To ensure you come home with all your fingers, take full note of the *Horses Bite and Kick* signs. These superstar animals are bred for high spirits—and are far too feisty to pet.

Other Sights: Visitors with extra time can explore three more attractions (all included in your entry ticket). The tranquil and photogenic **Japanese Gardens** were created by the colonel to depict the trials of life (beware the Tunnel of Ignorance). A wander through the more extensive and natural **St. Fiachra's Garden** (the patron saint of gardening) demands more time. Equestrian buffs may want to linger among the memorabilia in the small **Horse Museum,** where you can get a grip on how many hands it takes to measure a horse.

PRACTICALITIES

This section covers just the basics on traveling in the Republic of Ireland (for much more information, see *Rick Steves Ireland*). You'll find free advice on specific topics at www.ricksteves.com/tips.

Money

Ireland uses the euro currency: 1 euro (€) = about $1.20. To convert prices in euros to dollars, add about 20 percent: €20 = about $24, €50 = about $60. (Check www.oanda.com for the latest exchange rates.)

The standard way for travelers to get euros is to withdraw money from an ATM (which locals may call a "cash point") using a debit card, ideally with a Visa or MasterCard logo. To keep your cash, cards, and valuables safe, wear a money belt.

Before departing, call your bank or credit-card company: Confirm that your card(s) will work overseas, ask about international transaction fees, and alert them that you'll be making withdrawals in Europe. Also ask for the PIN number for your credit card—you may need it for Europe's "chip-and-PIN" payment machines (see below; allow time for your bank to mail your PIN to you).

Dealing with "Chip and PIN": Most credit and debit cards now have chips that authenticate and secure transactions. European cardholders insert their chip card into the payment slot, then enter a PIN. (For most US cards, you provide a signature.) Any American card, whether with a chip or an old-fashioned magnetic stripe, will work at Europe's hotels, restaurants, and shops. But some self-service chip-and-PIN payment machines—such as those at train stations, toll roads, or unattended gas pumps—may not accept your card, even if you know the PIN. If your card won't work, look for a cashier who can process the transaction manually—or pay in cash.

Dynamic Currency Conversion: If merchants or hoteliers offer to convert your purchase price into dollars (called dynamic currency conversion, or DCC), refuse this "service." You'll pay extra in fees for the expensive convenience of seeing your charge in dollars. If an ATM offers to "lock in" or "guarantee" your conversion rate, choose "proceed without conversion." Other prompts might state, "You can be charged in dollars: Press YES for dollars, NO for euros." Always choose the local currency.

Staying Connected

The simplest solution is to bring your own device—mobile phone, tablet, or laptop—and use it just as you would at home (following the tips below, such as connecting to free Wi-Fi whenever possible).

To call Ireland from a US or Canadian number: Whether you're phoning from a landline, your own mobile phone, or a Skype account, you're making an international call. Dial 011-353 and then the area code (minus its initial zero) and local number. (The 011 is our international access code, and 353 is Ireland's country code.) If dialing from a mobile phone, you can enter + in place of the international access code—press and hold the 0 key.

To call Ireland from a European country: Dial 00-353 followed by the area code (minus its initial zero) and local number. (The 00 is Europe's international access code.)

To call within Ireland: If you're dialing from a phone number within the same area code (for example, from a local landline), just dial the local number. If you're calling outside your area code (for example, from a mobile phone), dial both the area code (which starts with a 0) and the local number.

To call from Ireland to another country: Dial 00 followed by the country code (for example, 1 for the US or Canada), then the area code and number. If you're calling European countries whose phone numbers begin with 0, you'll usually have to omit that 0 when you dial.

Tips: If you bring your own mobile phone, consider getting an international plan; most providers offer a global calling plan that cuts the per-minute cost of phone calls and texts, and a flat-fee data plan.

Use Wi-Fi whenever possible. Most hotels and many cafés offer free Wi-Fi, and you'll likely also find it at tourist information offices, major museums, and public-transit hubs. With Wi-Fi you can use your phone or tablet to make free or inexpensive domestic and international calls via a calling app such as Skype, FaceTime,

Sleep Code

Hotels are classified based on the average price of an en suite double room with breakfast in high season.

$$$$	**Splurge:** Most rooms over €170
$$$	**Pricier:** €130-170
$$	**Moderate:** €90-130
$	**Budget:** €50-90
¢	**Backpacker:** Under €50
RS%	**Rick Steves discount**

Unless otherwise noted, credit cards are accepted and free Wi-Fi is available; at B&Bs, you'll likely need to pay cash. Comparison-shop by checking prices at several hotels (on each hotel's own website, on a booking site, or by email). For the best deal, book directly with the hotel. If the listing includes **RS%,** request a Rick Steves discount.

or Google+ Hangouts. When you can't find Wi-Fi, you can use your cellular network to connect to the Internet, send texts, or make voice calls. When you're done, avoid further charges by manually switching off "data roaming" or "cellular data."

It's possible to stay connected without a mobile device. You can make calls from your hotel (or the increasingly rare public phone), and check email or browse websites using public computers. Most hotels charge a high fee for international calls—ask for rates before you dial. For more on phoning, see www.ricksteves.com/phoning. For a one-hour talk on "Traveling with a Mobile Device," see www.ricksteves.com/travel-talks.

Sleeping

I've categorized my recommended accommodations based on price, indicated with a dollar-sign rating (see sidebar). I recommend reserving rooms in advance, particularly during peak season. Once your dates are set, check the specific price for your preferred stay at several hotels. You can do this either by comparing prices on Hotels.com or Booking.com, or by checking the hotels' own websites. To get the best deal, contact my family-run hotels directly by phone or email. When you go direct, the owner avoids any third-party commission, giving them wiggle room to offer you a discount, a nicer room, or free breakfast. If you prefer to book online or are considering a hotel chain, it's to your advantage to use the hotel's website.

For complicated requests, send an email with the following information: number and type of rooms; number of nights; arrival date; departure date; and any special requests. Use the European style for writing dates: day/month/year. Hoteliers typically ask for your credit-card number as a deposit. The prices I list include a

Restaurant Price Code

I've assigned each eatery a price category, based on the average cost of a typical main course. Drinks, desserts, and splurge items (steak and seafood) can raise the price considerably.

$$$$	**Splurge:** Most main courses over €25
$$$	**Pricier:** €20-25
$$	**Moderate:** €15-20
$	**Budget:** Under €15

In the Republic of Ireland, carryout fish-and-chips and other takeout food is **$**; a basic pub or sit-down eatery is **$$**; a gastropub or casual but more upscale restaurant is **$$$**; and a swanky splurge is **$$$$**.

hearty breakfast (unless otherwise noted).

Know the terminology: An "en suite" room has a bathroom (toilet and shower/tub) actually inside the room; a room with a "private bathroom" can mean that the bathroom is all yours, but it's across the hall. Guests in a "standard" room have access to a bathroom that's shared with other rooms and down the hall.

Some hotels are willing to make a deal to attract guests: Try emailing several hotels to ask for their best price. In general, hotel prices can soften if you do any of the following: stay in a "standard" room, offer to pay cash, stay at least three nights, or travel off-season.

Eating

I've categorized my recommended eateries based on price, indicated with a dollar-sign rating (see sidebar). The traditional "Irish Fry" breakfast includes juice, tea or coffee, cereal, eggs, bacon, sausage, toast, a grilled tomato, sautéed mushrooms, and black pudding. If that's too much for you, just order the items you want.

To dine affordably at classier restaurants, look for "early-bird specials" (offered about 17:30–19:00, last order by 19:00).

Smart travelers use pubs (short for "public houses") to eat, drink, and make new friends. Pub grub is Ireland's best eating value. For about $15–20, you'll get a basic hot lunch or dinner. The menu is hearty and traditional: stews, soups, fish-and-chips, meat, cabbage, potatoes, and—in coastal areas—fresh seafood. Order drinks and meals at the bar. Pay as you order, and don't tip.

When you say "a beer, please" in an Irish pub, you'll get a pint of Guinness. (If you think you don't like Guinness, try it in Ireland.) For a cold, refreshing, basic, American-style beer, ask for a lager, such as Harp. If you want a small beer, ask for a glass or a half-pint.

Craic (pronounced crack), Irish for "fun" or "a good laugh," means good conversation for the participants. It's the sport that accompanies drinking in a pub. People are there to talk. Don't be afraid to make new friends. To toast them in Irish, say, *"Slainte"* (SLAWN-chuh).

Traditional music is alive and popular in pubs throughout Ireland. "Sessions" (musical evenings) may be planned and advertised or impromptu. There's generally a fiddle, a flute or tin whistle, a guitar, a *bodhrán* (goatskin drum), and maybe an accordion or mandolin. Things usually get going at about 21:30. Last call for drinks is at about 23:30.

Tipping: At a sit-down place with table service, tip about 10 percent—unless the service charge is already listed on the bill. If you order at a counter, there's no need to tip.

Transportation

By Car: A car is a worthless headache in Dublin. But if venturing into the countryside, I enjoy the freedom of a rental car for reaching far-flung rural sights. It's cheaper to arrange most car rentals from the US. Note that many credit-card companies do not offer collision coverage for rentals in Ireland. For tips on your insurance options, see www.ricksteves.com/cdw, and for route planning, consult www.viamichelin.com. Bring your driver's license. In the Republic of Ireland, you generally can't rent a car if you're 75 or older (unless you have a note from your doctor), and you'll pay extra if you're 70-74.

Remember that the Irish drive on the left side of the road (and the driver sits on the right side of the car). You'll quickly master Ireland's many roundabouts: Traffic moves clockwise, cars inside the roundabout have the right-of-way, and entering traffic yields (look to your right as you merge). Note that "camera cops" strictly enforce speed limits by automatically snapping photos of speeders' license plates, then mailing them a bill. Also be aware that your US credit and debit cards with a chip may not work at self-service gas pumps and automated parking garages—but if you know your PIN, try it anyway. The easiest solution is carrying sufficient cash.

The M-50 ring road surrounding Dublin carries a €3.10 toll, paid electronically with an eFlow pass. Get details from your rental-car company.

Local road etiquette is similar to that in the US. Ask your car-rental company for details, or check the US State Department website (www.travel.state.gov, search for Ireland in the "Learn about your destination" box, then click on "Travel and Transportation").

By Train and Bus: You can check train schedules at www.irishrail.ie or listen to a recorded timetable at 01/890-778-899. In

Ireland, most travelers find it's cheapest simply to buy train tickets as they go. To see if a rail pass could save you money, check www.ricksteves.com/rail.

Long-distance buses (called "coaches") are about a third slower than trains, but they're also much cheaper. Bus stations are normally at or near train stations. The Bus Éireann Expressway Bus Timetable is handy (free, available at some bus stations or online at www.buseireann.ie, bus info tel. 1850-836-611).

Helpful Hints

Emergency Help: To summon the **police** or an **ambulance,** dial 999. For passport problems, call the **US Embassy** (in Dublin, tel. 01/630-6200) or the **Canadian Embassy** (in Dublin, tel. 01/234-4000). For other concerns, get advice from your hotelier.

Theft or Loss: To replace a passport, you'll need to go in person to an embassy or consulate (see above). Cancel and replace your credit and debit cards by calling these 24-hour US numbers collect: Visa—tel. 303/967-1096, MasterCard—tel. 636/722-7111, American Express—tel. 336/393-1111. In Ireland, to make a collect call to the US, dial 1-800-550-000; press zero or stay on the line for an operator. File a police report either on the spot or within a day or two; you'll need it to submit an insurance claim for lost or stolen rail passes or electronics, and it can help with replacing your passport or credit and debit cards. For more information, see www.ricksteves.com/help.

Time: Ireland uses the 24-hour clock. It's the same through 12:00 noon, then keep going: 13:00, 14:00, and so on. Ireland, like Great Britain, is five/eight hours ahead of the East/West Coasts of the US (and one hour earlier than most of continental Europe).

Holidays and Festivals: Ireland celebrates many holidays, which can close sights and attract crowds (book hotel rooms ahead). For information on holidays and festivals, check Ireland's tourism website: www.discoverireland.com. For a simple list showing major—though not all—events, see www.ricksteves.com/festivals.

Numbers and Stumblers: What Americans call the second floor of a building is the first floor in Ireland. Irish people write dates as day/month/year, so Christmas 2019 is 25/12/19. For most measurements, Ireland uses the metric system: A kilogram is 2.2 pounds, a liter is about a quart, and a kilometer is six-tenths of a mile.

Resources from Rick Steves

This Snapshot guide is excerpted from my latest edition of *Rick Steves Ireland,* one of many titles in my ever-expanding series of guidebooks on European travel. I also produce a public television series, *Rick Steves' Europe,* and a public radio show, *Travel with Rick Steves.* My website, www.ricksteves.com, offers free travel information, a forum for travelers' comments, guidebook updates, my travel blog, an online travel store, and information on European rail passes and our tours of Europe. If you're bringing a mobile device, my free Rick Steves Audio Europe app features dozens of self-guided audio tours of the top sights in Europe and travel interviews about Ireland. You can get Rick Steves Audio Europe via Apple's App Store, Google Play, or the Amazon Appstore. For more information, see www.ricksteves.com/audioeurope.

Additional Resources

Tourist Information: www.discoverireland.com
Passports and Red Tape: www.travel.state.gov
Packing List: www.ricksteves.com/packing
Travel Insurance: www.ricksteves.com/insurance
Cheap Flights: www.kayak.com or www.google.com/flights
Airplane Carry-on Restrictions: www.tsa.gov/travelers
Updates for This Book: www.ricksteves.com/update

How Was Your Trip?

To share your tips, concerns, and discoveries after using this book, please fill out the survey at www.ricksteves.com/feedback. Thanks in advance—it helps a lot.

INDEX

INDEX

Explore Europe

At ricksteves.com you can browse through thousands of articles, videos, photos and radio interviews, plus find a wealth of money-saving travel tips for planning your dream trip. And with our mobile-friendly website, you can easily access all this great travel information anywhere you go.

TV Shows

Preview the places you'll visit by watching entire half-hour episodes of Rick Steves' Europe (choose from all 100 shows) on-demand, for free.

your travel dreams into affordable reality

Radio Interviews

Enjoy ready access to Rick's vast library of radio interviews covering travel

tips and cultural insights that relate specifically to your Europe travel plans.

Travel Forums

Learn, ask, share! Our online community of savvy travelers is a great resource for first-time travelers to Europe, as well as seasoned pros. You'll find forums on each country, plus travel tips and restaurant/hotel reviews. You can even ask one of our well-traveled staff to chime in with an opinion.

Travel News

Subscribe to our free Travel News e-newsletter, and get monthly updates from Rick on what's happening in Europe.

Rick's Free Travel App

Get your FREE **Rick Steves Audio Europe**™ app to enjoy…

- Dozens of self-guided tours of Europe's top museums, sights and historic walks
- Hundreds of tracks filled with cultural insights and sightseeing tips from Rick's radio interviews
- All organized into handy geographic playlists
- For Apple and Android

With Rick whispering in your ear, Europe gets even better.

Find out more at ricksteves.com

Gear up for your next adventure at ricksteves.com

Light Luggage

Pack light and right with Rick Steves' affordable, custom-designed rolling carry-on bags, backpacks, day packs and shoulder bags.

Accessories

From packing cubes to moneybelts and beyond, Rick has personally selected the travel goodies that will help your trip go smoother.

Rick Steves has

Experience maximum Europe

Save time and energy

This guidebook is your independent-travel toolkit. But for all it delivers, it's still up to you to devote the time and energy it takes to manage the preparation and logistics that are essential for a happy trip. If that's a hassle, there's a solution.

Rick Steves Tours

A Rick Steves tour takes you to Europe's most interesting places with great

with minimum stress

guides and small groups of 28 or less. We follow Rick's favorite itineraries, ride in comfy buses, stay in family-run hotels, and bring you intimately

close to the Europe you've traveled so far to see. Most importantly, we take away the logistical headaches so you can focus on the fun.

Join the fun

This year we'll take thousands of free-spirited

travelers—nearly half of them repeat customers—along with us on four dozen different itineraries, from Ireland to Italy to Athens. Is a Rick Steves tour the right fit for your travel dreams? Find out at ricksteves.com, where you can also request Rick's latest tour catalog. Europe is best experienced with happy travel partners. We hope you can join us.

See our itineraries at ricksteves.com

BEST OF GUIDES

Full color easy-to-scan format, focusing on Europe's most popular destinations and sights.

Best of France
Best of Germany
Best of England
Best of Europe
Best of Ireland
Best of Italy
Best of Spain

COMPREHENSIVE GUIDES

City, country, and regional guides with detailed coverage for a multi-week trip exploring the most iconic sights and venturing off the beaten track.

Amsterdam & the Netherlands
Barcelona
Belgium: Bruges, Brussels,
  Antwerp & Ghent
Berlin
Budapest
Croatia & Slovenia
Eastern Europe
England
Florence & Tuscany
France
Germany
Great Britain
Greece: Athens & the Peloponnese
Iceland
Ireland
Istanbul
Italy
London
Paris
Portugal
Prague & the Czech Republic
Provence & the French Riviera
Rome
Scandinavia
Scotland
Spain
Switzerland
Venice
Vienna, Salzburg & Tirol

HE BEST OF ROME

he, Italy's capital, is studded with
an remnants and floodlit-fountain
res. From the Vatican to the Colos-
, with crazy traffic in between, Rome
derful, huge, and exhausting. The
s, the heat, and the weighty history

of the Eternal City where Caesars walked
can make tourists wilt. Recharge by taking siestas, gelato breaks, and after-dark
walks, strolling from one atmospheric
square to another in the refreshing evening air.

*l Pantheon—which
st done until the
y 2,000 years old
over 1,500).*

*f Athens in the Vat-
lies the humanistic
e.*

*adiators fought
nother, entertaining*

Rome ristorante.

*at St. Peter's
eriously*

toss in a coin

Rick Steves guidebooks are published by Avalon Travel,
an imprint of Perseus Books, a Hachette Book Group company.

POCKET GUIDES

Compact, full color city guides with the essentials for shorter trips.

Amsterdam
Athens
Barcelona
Florence
Italy's Cinque Terre
London
Munich & Salzburg

Paris
Prague
Rome
Venice
Vienna

SNAPSHOT GUIDES

Focused single-destination coverage.

Basque Country: Spain & France
Copenhagen & the Best of Denmark
Dublin
Dubrovnik
Edinburgh
Hill Towns of Central Italy
Krakow, Warsaw & Gdansk
Lisbon
Loire Valley
Madrid & Toledo
Milan & the Italian Lakes District
Naples & the Amalfi Coast
Northern Ireland
Normandy
Norway
Reykjavik
Sevilla, Granada & Southern Spain
St. Petersburg, Helsinki & Tallinn
Stockholm

CRUISE PORTS GUIDES

Reference for cruise ports of call.

Mediterranean Cruise Ports
Northern European Cruise Ports

Complete your library with...

TRAVEL SKILLS & CULTURE

Study up on travel skills and gain insight on history and culture.

Europe 101
European Christmas
European Easter
European Festivals
Europe Through the Back Door
Postcards from Europe
Travel as a Political Act

PHRASE BOOKS & DICTIONARIES

French
French, Italian & German
German
Italian
Portuguese
Spanish

PLANNING MAPS

Britain, Ireland & London
Europe
France & Paris
Germany, Austria & Switzerland
Ireland
Italy
Spain & Portugal

Avalon Travel
Hachette Book Group
1700 Fourth Street
Berkeley, CA 94710

Printed in Canada by Friesens.
First printing January 2018.

Fifth Edition
ISBN 978-1-63121-683-1

For the latest on Rick's lectures, guidebooks, tours, public television series, and public radio show, contact Rick Steves' Europe, 130 Fourth Avenue North, Edmonds, WA 98020, tel. 425/771-8303, www.ricksteves.com, rick@ricksteves.com.

Rick Steves' Europe

Managing Editor: Jennifer Madison Davis
Special Publications Manager: Risa Laib
Assistant Managing Editor: Cathy Lu
Editors: Glenn Eriksen, Tom Griffin, Katherine Gustafson, Suzanne Kotz, Rosie Leutzinger, Carrie Shepherd
Editorial & Production Assistant: Jessica Shaw
Editorial Intern: Claire Connor
Contributor: Gene Openshaw
Graphic Content Director: Sandra Hundacker
Maps & Graphics: David C. Hoerlein, Lauren Mills, Mary Rostad

Avalon Travel

Senior Editor and Series Manager: Madhu Prasher
Editor: Jamie Andrade
Associate Editor: Sierra Machado
Copy Editor: Denise Silva
Proofreaders: Patrick Collins, Patty Mon
Indexer: Stephen Callahan
Production & Typesetting: Krista Anderson, Lisi Baldwin, Rue Flaherty, Christine DeLorenzo
Cover Design: Kimberly Glyder Design
Maps & Graphics: Kat Bennett

Photo Credits

Front Cover: Temple Bar, Dublin © Attila Tatár | Dreamstime
Title Page: © Rich Earl
Additional Photography: Dominic Arizona Bonuccelli, Rich Earl, Trish Feaster, David C. Hoerlein, Pat O'Connor, Rick Steves, Wikimedia Commons (PD-Art/PD-US). Photos are used by permission and are the property of the original copyright owners.

Although every effort was made to ensure that the information was correct at the time of going to press, the author and publisher do not assume and hereby disclaim any liability to any party for any loss or damage caused by errors, omissions, loathsome leprechauns, or any potential travel disruption due to labor or financial difficulty, whether such errors or omissions result from negligence, accident, or any other cause.

ABOUT THE AUTHORS

RICK STEVES

Since 1973, Rick has spent about four months a year exploring Europe. His mission: to empower Americans to have European trips that are fun, affordable, and culturally broadening. Rick produces a best-selling guidebook series, a public television series, and a public radio show, and organizes small-group tours that take over 20,000 travelers to Europe annually. He does all of this with the help of a hardworking, well-traveled staff of 100 at Rick Steves' Europe in Edmonds, Washington, near Seattle. When not on the road, Rick is active in his church and with advocacy groups focused on economic justice, drug policy reform, and ending hunger. To recharge, Rick plays piano, relaxes at his family cabin in the Cascade Mountains, and spends time with his partner Trish, son Andy, and daughter Jackie. Find out more about Rick at www.ricksteves.com and on Facebook.

PAT O'CONNOR

Pat O'Connor, an Irish-American, first journeyed to Ireland in 1981 and was hooked by the history and passion of the feisty Irish culture. Frequent return visits led to his partnership with Rick, his work as an Ireland tour guide for Rick Steves' Europe, and co-authorship of this book. Pat, who loves all things Hibernian except the black pudding, thrives on the adventures that occur as he slogs the bogs and drives the Irish back lanes (over 2,000 kilometers annually) in search of new discoveries.

More for your trip!
Maximize the experience with Rick Steves as your guide

Guidebooks
Make side trips smooth and affordable with Rick's England and Scotland guides

Planning Maps
Use Rick's pre-trip planning tool for mapping out your itinerary

Rick's TV Shows
Preview your destinations with a variety of shows covering Ireland

Rick's Audio Europe™ App
Get free travel information for Ireland

Small Group Tours
Take a lively, low-stress Rick Steves tour through Ireland

For all the details, visit ricksteves.com